For The Love Of AUSTRIA

CHRISTIAN J. FISCHER

Copyright © 2020 Author: Christian J. Fischer

All rights reserved. No part of this publication may be reproduced, distributed, or transmitted in any form or by any means, including photocopying, recording, or other electronic or mechanical methods, without the prior written permission of the publisher or author, except in the case of brief quotations embodied in critical reviews and specific other noncommercial uses permitted by copyright law. For permission requests, email the publisher or author at (info@christianjfischer.com) or send your request to Publishing request, 934 Chamberlain Highway, Suite 1001, Kensington CT 06037.

ISBN-10: 1544724063

ISBN-13: 978-1544724065

Printed in the United States of America

FOREWORD

Chef Christian has succeeded in every chef's goal – evoking memories. "For The Love of Austria" will permit all cooks to create new memories, and will rekindle memories of home, family, and familiar food for all readers of Austrio-German heritage. My mother immigrated from Germany and that meant we regularly ate *Greissknockerlsuppe, Gurkensalat, Wiener Schnitzel, Semmelknoedel,* and many others dishes presented in this book.

My years cooking in Germany permitted me to eat and cook all these mouthwatering dishes in Chef Christian's book. While I worked with chefs who prepared many of the dishes in "For The Love of Austria", I learned more than how to cook the food. I also learned the great pride in the traditions and heritage of these dishes. Chef Christian has professionally captured these timeless recipes and made them attainable to everyone.

"For The Love of Austria" will be a cookbook you will reach for over and over again. The dishes span the seasons and will be delicious at any meal. My dear friend, Chef Christian, has made the food of Austria easy to cook for everyone.

Sincerely,
Ron DeSantis
Certified Master Chef

DEDICATION

This book is dedicated to my family.
Jennifer, your passion warmed me;
Ting, your words of encouragement inspired me;
Margie, Caleb & Stefan, your constant support guided me;

I love you!

CONTENTS

	Acknowledgments	Pg. 1
1	About Austria *Facts / Figures / Culinary History*	Pg. 2
2	Soups	Pg. 24
3	Salads	Pg. 40
4	Side Dishes	Pg. 60
5	Entrées	Pg. 76
6	Desserts	Pg. 96
8	About the Author	Pg. 120
9	References	Pg. 121
10	Index	Pg. 122

Underneath each recipe, you will find a picture of a whisk. I thought I needed to give you a heads up on the culinary complexity of each dish. The amounts of whisk will allow you to schedule extra time for a recipe based on the quantities of whisks it has.

ONE = This is going to be fun and delicious!
TWO = You can do this!
THREE = No crying allowed!

Enjoy, have fun, and celebrate the culture I am very proud of.

ACKNOWLEDGMENTS

First and foremost, I would like to thank my wife, Jennifer, for standing beside me throughout my career and writing this book. She has been my inspiration and motivation for continuing to improve my knowledge and move my career forward. She is my rock, and I dedicate this book to her. I also thank my beautiful children: Stefan, Ting, Margie, and our new addition Caleb, for always making me smile and for understanding on those weekend mornings when I was writing this book instead of playing games. I hope that one day they can read this book and understand why I spent so much time in the kitchen and in front of my computer. I'd like to thank my parents and grandparents for allowing me to follow my ambitions throughout my childhood. My family, including my in-laws, have always supported me throughout my career and authoring this book, and I appreciate it.

I look forward to discussing this book with my family and friends at future gatherings as I'm sure they will all read it soon. My co-workers and mentors, who showed me the ropes and always challenged me to do better and write about Austria, which ultimately led to this!

A special "Thank You" to Jeanette Gumbulevich for always trying my new recipes and Austrian heritage infused beverages with such joy and celebration. In the end, I believe that the support of all my friends and family provides the perfect blend of encouragement and motivation that went into authoring this book. I think that it will be a great asset to the culinary community! Thanks for everything. I look forward to writing the second edition soon!

Please enjoy my **"Love Letter to Austria"** and this trip into a rich culinary culture I am very proud of.

ABOUT AUSTRIA
Facts / Figures / History / culinary history

Austria is a landlocked country of approximately 8.7 million inhabitants in Central Europe. It is bordered by the Czech Republic and Germany to the north, Slovakia and Hungary to the east, Slovenia and Italy to the south, and Switzerland and Liechtenstein to the west. The territory of Austria covers 83,878 square kilometers (32,385 sq. mi) and has a temperate and alpine climate. Austria's terrain is highly mountainous due to the presence of the Alps; only 32% of the country is below 500 meters (1,640 ft.), and ad its highest point, the Grossglockner is 3,798 meters (12,460 ft.). The majority of the population speaks German, which is also the country's official language. Other local official languages are Croatian, Hungarian and Slovene.

The capital and largest city, with a population exceeding 1.8 million, is Vienna. Austria is one of the wealthiest countries in the world, with a nominal per capita GDP of $51,480 (2017 est.). The country has developed a high standard of living and, in 2016, was ranked 21st in the world for its Human Development Index. Austria has been a member of the United Nations since 1955, joined the European Union in 1995, and is a founder of the OECD. Austria also signed the Schengen Agreement in 1995 and adopted the European currency, the euro, in 1999.

As a federal republic, Austria is comprised of nine independent federal states or provinces: Burgenland, Carinthia, Lower Austria, Upper Austria, Salzburg, Styria, Tyrol, Vorarlberg, and Vienna.

Austria has a strong economy with machinery, metallurgical products, and textiles being of particular importance. The country's most important

AUSTRIAN HISTORY

The origins of Austria date back to the time of the Roman Empire when a Celtic kingdom was conquered by the Romans in approximately 15 BC and later became Noricum, a Roman province, in the mid 1st century AD—an area which mostly encloses today's Austria. In 788 AD, the Frankish king Charlemagne conquered the area and introduced Christianity. Under the native Habsburg dynasty, Austria became one of the great powers of Europe. In 1867, the Austrian Empire was reformed into Austria-Hungary.

The Austro-Hungarian Empire collapsed in 1918 with the end of World War I. The First Austrian Republic was established in 1919. In the 1938 Anschluss, Austria was occupied and annexed by Nazi Germany. This lasted until the end of World War II in 1945, after which the Allies occupied Austria, and its former democratic constitution was restored. In 1955, the Austrian State Treaty re-established Austria as a sovereign state, ending the occupation. In the same year, the Austrian Parliament created the Declaration of Neutrality, which declared that the country would become permanently neutral.

The Habsburg Empire stretched from the borders of Imperial Russia to the Adriatic and consisted of more than a dozen nationalities, with over 51 million people speaking sixteen different languages. Within the last seven centuries, the cosmopolitan Habsburg rule extended over Switzerland, Alsace, Burgundy, Spain, Holland, Bohemia, Moravia, Slovakia, Poland, Hungary, Croatia, Slovenia, and Italy. All of the above have influenced Austria's unique cuisine in their own way with ingredients and culinary craftsmanship.

Austria is famous for its castles, palaces, and buildings, among other architectural works. Some of Austria's most famous castles include Festung Hohensalzburg, Burg Hohenwerfen, Castle Liechtenstein, and the Schloß Artstetten. Many of Austria's castles were created during the Habsburg reign.

The Historic Centre of the City of Salzburg was listed as a World Heritage Site in 1996, stating that "Salzburg had managed to preserve an extraordinarily rich urban fabric, developed over the period from the Middle Ages to the 19th century when it was a city-state ruled by a prince-archbishop."

Three years later, the City of Graz - Historic Centre followed Salzburg, as the "old city is a harmonious blend of the architectural styles and artistic movements that have succeeded each other since the Middle Ages, together with cultural influences from the neighboring regions."

In 2001, finally, the Historic Centre of Vienna was listed as World Heritage Site, with the comment that the "historic center of Vienna is rich in architectural ensembles, including Baroque castles and gardens, as well as the late-19th-century Ringstrasse lined with grand buildings, monument's and parks." The country's culture is intricately intertwined with people's love for nature and music. Austria has been home to some of the most famous musicians and composers in the world, with Austrians taking great pride in their musical heritage.

AUSTRIAN CULTURE

Austrian culture has been greatly influenced not only by the Habsburg imperial family but also by its neighbors. Vienna has long been considered the music capital of Europe and is home to world-class music schools. Famous composers such as Johann Strauss, Joseph Hayden, and Wolfgang Amadeus Mozart all learned, composed, taught, and played in Vienna. This means that Vienna is also home to some of the best venues on the planet, such as the Golden Hall, the Vienna State Opera, and the Musikverein, to name a few. There is always something going on in the music scene in Vienna, including numerous festivals.
Also, home to the Alps and great outdoor sports, Austria has many world-class athletes. With all the peaks to conquer, it is no surprise that some of the globe's

top mountaineers are Austrian, including Peter Aufschnaiter, Heinrich Harrer, and Ludwig Purtscheller. Great Austrian skiers include Toni Sailer, Franz Klammer, and Hermann Meier. Austria's lengthy military history has created a long partnership with horses, and the Spanish Riding School in Vienna stands at the pinnacle of horsemanship in the world.

Being a land-locked country, Austria is bordered by the Czech Republic, Germany, Hungary, Slovakia, Slovenia, Italy, Switzerland, and Liechtenstein. This means that Austrians are open to a diverse range of cultures, religions, and languages. Although German is the official language, most Austrians are multi-lingual. Depending on the region in which they live, Austrians may speak Italian, Turkish, or Serbian, as well as regional Austrian dialects and English.

LANGUAGE

Schoolchildren in Austria are taught to read and write in Standard German (Standarddeutsch, Hochdeutsch), which is the language of business and government in Austria. The Austrian German spoken at home and in local commerce will be one of many regional Upper German dialects (either Austro-Bavarian or Alemannic dialects).

While strong forms of the various dialects are not commonly comprehensible to other native German speakers such as Germans or
Swiss, there is virtually no communication barrier between the Austro-Bavarian dialects in Austria and those in Bavaria, Germany. The Central Austro-Bavarian dialects are more intelligible to speakers of Standard German than the Southern Austro-Bavarian dialects of Tyrol. Viennese, the Austro-Bavarian dialect of Vienna, is most frequently used in Germany for impersonations of the typical inhabitant of Austria. The people of Graz, the capital of Styria, speak yet another dialect which is not very Styrian and more easily understood by people from other parts of Austria than different Styrian dialects, e.g., from western

Styria. As for Western Austria, the dialect of the state of Vorarlberg and a small piece of North Tyrol has linguistically and culturally more in common with German-speaking Switzerland and Baden-Württemberg or Swabia in Southwest Germany as it is an Alemannic dialect like Swiss German or Swabian German.

Bilingual German-Hungarian sign in Oberwart, Burgenland. As part of its historical, cultural heritage of being a multinational state for centuries (Habsburg Monarchy, Austrian Empire, later Austria-Hungary), modern Austria is not entirely homogenously German speaking. Still, it has within its borders, albeit small, autochthonous minorities of the different native tongue: Hungarian is the most widely spoken of the recognized minority languages spoken in Austria (mostly in Burgenland, where it is an official language, and in Vienna; about 40,000 speakers (0.5% of the Austrian population)). Slovene (24,000) has the same status in Carinthia and Styria. The same is true for Burgenland Croatian (19,000), a variant of Croatian spoken in Burgenland. Furthermore, Czech (18,000), Slovak (10,000), and Romani (6,000) are recognized based on minority rights protection.

Austrian German, especially the Viennese dialect, has taken over some words from Hungarian, Czech, Yiddish or some South Slavic languages to replace words otherwise used in Standard German (such as Maschekseitn (the other side), from the Hungarian a másik (the other one), Standard German die andere Seite).

THE SALT OF THE EARTH

Visit one of the oldest salt mines in the world at Hallein near Salzburg; its salt provided a livelihood for local people, brought riches to the archbishops, and built the magnificent city of Salzburg we admire today.
Hunter-gatherers first discovered salty mountain springs, and underground salt mining in this region dates back to the Celts. Salt enabled people to preserve

food and give it flavor. Centuries later, the archbishops, rulers of Salzburg, took over the lucrative salt trade and, with the profits developed it into an opulent, baroque residence.

Since 1994 the historic salt mines in Hallein have been open only as a show mine. Austria's salt supply still comes from these mountains, but from Altaussee, where the source from an ancient sea has lasted for more than 250 million years.

Your journey into the history of Hallein's salt mines begins with a comfortable train ride into the mountain, where experienced miners guide you and explain the mining process. You will also enjoy a raft ride across an underground lake and an exciting descent on two mining slides.

The tunnel system is maintained to prevent the mountain from sinking. Of the original 40 miles of mining tunnels, which pass through 21 horizons, as the underground levels are called, about 7 miles and nine horizons can still be accessed.

The pride of the miners of Hallein and their close links to life underground is much in evidence when they perform their Sword Dance. Hallein's miners perform this dance, which dates back to 1586, in uniform with boots and carrying a sword, which was a privilege bestowed on them by law in 1405. The dance, which is performed by more than 80 miners, lasts about an hour and symbolizes various working practices underground. It is performed at night by the light of torches and to the music of the miners' brass band.

Venerated as a "gift of the gods," traded like gold: This natural resource shaped the history of Austria in general, and the areas surrounding the city of Salzburg in particular. Cities such as Salzburg, Hallein and Hallstatt, as well as regions like the Salzkammergut owe their names, but also their prosperity, to salt.

AUSTRIAN TRADITIONS

One thing to understand about Austrian food culture is that in Austria, food is relished, and meals are celebrated. Austrians can spend more than an hour discussing various topics over a meal and afterward spend an equal amount of time to finish their conversations over a cup of coffee and dessert. This behavior is often referred to as typical Austrian Gemuetlichkeit and is distinctive to Austrian culture. Gemuetlichkeit, a word that has been adopted in the English language, describes an environment or state of mind that produces a happy mood and a sense of well-being. It represents a notion of belonging and social acceptance, of being cozy and welcoming. That is precisely what you would expect to find in most of Austria's local taverns, restaurants, and cafés. In this section, we show you where Austrians love to spend their time during the year.

CHRISTKINDLMARKT

Visiting one of the many Christkindlmärkte (Christmas markets) in Austria is a popular tradition during the four weeks of Advent. Christkindlmärkte can be described as street markets that sell Christmas ornaments, cookies, and other things related to Christmas. Apart from shopping, people like to enjoy a Glühwein, Punsch, and many other festive delicacies.

FOOD

Austrian cuisine, which is often incorrectly equated with Viennese cuisine, is derived from the cuisine of the Austro-Hungarian Empire. In addition to native regional traditions, it has been influenced above all by Hungarian, Jewish, and hands Italian cooking, from which both dishes and methods of food preparation have often been borrowed. Goulash is one example of this. Austrian cuisine is known primarily in the rest of the world for its pastries and sweets. In recent times a new regional cuisine has also developed, which is center locational produce and employs modern and comfortable methods of preparation.

Every state in Austria has some specialties: In Lower Austria, they have poppies, in Burgenland polenta, in Styria pumpkin, in Carinthia's many lakes they have fish, in Upper Austria, dumpling play a vital role, for Salzburg the Salzburger Nockerln are famous (a Soufflé), Tyrol has their Tyrolean bacon, and Vorarlberg is influenced by the close neighbors Switzerland and the Swabia region in Germany; thus, cheese plays a role, and cheesy Swabian Spätzle is a specialty there.

But not all of what can be enjoyed at Austria's restaurants and cafés nowadays has peacefully found its way into Austria's kitchens. Many recipes and ingredients had been washed ashore by Austria's melting pot of pan-european cooking by accident or as a coincidence or war. The Turkish invasion of Europe, for example, heralded the birth of Austria's coffee culture by introducing the coffee bean to Viennese cooks. Furthermore, "Apfelstrudel" is an Austrian version of a Turkish delicacy introduced during the Turkish occupation. The Wiener Schnitzel probably originated in northern Italy, while the delicious Palatschinken (crêpes) and the Gulasch came from the Hungarian plains; the roasts and sausages were originally Southern German delicacies, the pastries originated in Bohemia.

Apart from the foreign influences on Austrian cuisine, every Austrian feature their own local dishes: Frittatensuppe (crêpe soup) comes from Styria, Speckknödel (bacon dumplings) from Tyrol; and Salzburg, Mozart's home, has contributed the so-called Salzburger Nockerln, a sweet soufflé made from eggs and finished with long-established culinary proficiency.

EATING WITH AUSTRIANS

When having a meal as a group, it is polite to wish one another 'Guten Appetit' or 'Mahlzeit.' Mahlzeit means 'mealtime' and is also used as a general greeting around midday when one can assume that most people are about to have lunch.
At traditional restaurants, especially in the countryside, it is considered polite to greet other punters with a hearty 'Mahlzeit.' A typical Austrian meal can be a long-running affair, as there are generally at least three courses and no rush to leave after the last bite. It is common to languish at the table and enjoy a drink before relinquishing the table to the next party.

DRINKING WITH AUSTRIANS

When clinking glasses, Austrians take a moment to make eye contact and say 'Prost' to each person in the round. If you feel like showing off, you can also say 'Zum Wohl' or 'Prosit' - all three mean 'to your health.'
Skiing instructors, tour guides, bartenders, and otherwise well-informed Austrians will be more than happy to teach you a variety of less formal, usually rowdy toasts that are popular throughout the country. Austria's excellent wines, beers, and spirits are the pride of local restaurateurs, so make sure to sample regional beverages whenever possible.
After a meal, you are likely to be offered a shot of Schnaps, Austria's favorite digestive. This is not a drink for the faint-hearted: the rule is to drink it in a single mouthful and, with most varieties containing around 40% alcohol, this is – literally – an eye-watering experience.

HEURIGER

It was Austrian Emperor Joseph II in the 18th century who issued a decree that permitted all residents to open establishments to sell and serve self-produced wine, juices, and other food and snacks. Until the 20th century, it was quite customary for guests to bring along their own food to go with the wine they drank at the tavern, now known as Heuriger. Heurig means most recent in German, and at a Heuriger, the most recent wine is served. Heuriger is one of the most popular and most frequented places, Austrians like to go to during the Spring, Summer, and Autumn months to experience Gemuetlichkeit. Typical foods and drinks that are served at a Heuriger include Brettljause (a variation of cheese, sausages, and spreads) and Liptauer (a spread flavored with pepper, wine, and must (a kind of apple cider).

CHEESE CULTURE

Enjoying light cuisine with ease – that's what makes Austria's master cheesemakers so successful. Their spirit of innovation transforms cream cheese into unique cream cheese creations made from cow's, sheep's and goat's milk, exotically combined with herbs, fruits, or vegetables. In the process, each region offers its own specialties, which are often based upon century-old recipes and have been adapted to suit the spirit of the times. Austria's cream cheeses are wellness for the senses. They are light, capture the imagination, and caress the palate.

SOFT CHEESE

The creation of many soft cheese specialties dates back to the previous century when they were produced in the country's numerous monasteries. Whether with outer mold, inner mold, or red cultures, every recipe and every cheese has its own particular flavor. The nuances range from mild through to hearty robust. Various soft cheeses can be discovered in Upper Austria and Styria. They are manufactured in monasteries or small alpine dairies, which manage to develop unique creations. Depending upon the recipe and degree of ripening, the characteristic flavor ranges from mild-fine through to tangy-strong, tasty, but always exciting. The maturation occurs from the exterior through to the interior during a period of 2 to 4 weeks. The facets of the ripening could not be more different: From the white mold skin and red culture rind through to blue or green inner mold and double mold.

SEMI-HARD CHEESE

Austrian semi-hard cheese offers a diverse palette. Alongside classics such as Gouda and Tilsiter, every cheese fan has their personal favorite. The choice ranges from soft through to firm, from aromatic through to mild. Semi-hard cheese has centuries of tradition in Austria. Manufacturing is subsequently widespread throughout the country and often has a strong regional base. This is reflected in the names of the cheese; specialties such as Dachsteiner, Arlberger, or Gmundner Bergkäse are to be found here. Semi-hard cheeses are evenly ripened cheeses with a firm, smooth consistency and small slit- or grain-shaped eyes, or a broken eye formation. It depends upon the breaking strength of the cheese. Semi-hard cheese is the cheese style that features in most cheese types.

HARD CHEESE

Time and tradition are what distinguish the character and uniqueness of Austria's hard cheese. From a mild, fully aromatic taste through to a special piquancy. Thanks to the long storage, Emmentaler and Bergkäse have an incomparably natural flavor. Arlberg combines the intense, full aromatic cheese pleasure of Tyrol and Vorarlberg. Here you can become acquainted with a nature in which generations of mountain cows have been providing the fresh, pure milk for the typical tangy Bergkäse. This natural landscape extends an invitation for hiking or Nordic walking in the valleys and gorges, up to the high alpine pastures and mountain chalets and easily accessible panoramic viewpoints. The saying, "The way is the goal," is especially true here. And –

with their culinary delights – the many chalets en-route truly transform it into a pleasant hike!

VIENNESE CUISINE

Vienna has been the capital of Austria for more than a thousand years. It became the cultural center of the nation and developed its own regional cuisine; as such, Viennese Cuisine bears the unique distinction of being the only kind of cooking named after a city.
The variety of ingredients sold on the "Naschmarkt" might lead to the thought of a broadly varied cooking culture. In fact, dishes heavily depending on meat make up typical Viennese cuisine: Wiener schnitzel (veal coated in breadcrumbs and fried), "Tafelspitz" (boiled beef), "Beuschel" (a ragout containing veal lungs and heart), and "Selchfleisch" (smoked meat) with sauerkraut and dumplings are typical of its cooking.

Some sweet Viennese dishes include Apfelstrudel (strudel pastry filled with apples), "Millirahmstrudel" (milk-cream strudel), "Kaiserschmarrn" (shredded pancakes served with fruit compotes), and "Sachertorte" (cake of two layers of chocolate cake with apricot jam in the middle). These and many other desserts will be on offer at one of the many "Konditorei" of Vienna, where they are generally eaten with coffee in the afternoon. Liptauer as a spread, or Powidl also as spread or base for dumplings are also quite popular.

VIENNESE CAFÉ

The culture of coffee houses in the West began in Austria and remained a fixture of its culture. Much of the reputation these achieved during the turn of the 19th century resulted when writers like Peter Altenberg, Karl Kraus, Hermann Broch, and Friedrich Torberg decided to use them as places of work and socializing. Celebrated Austrian writer Peter Altenberg is rumored to have given "Wien 1, Café Central" as his private address, as he spent so much time in Café Central. Artists, thinkers, and political radicals of the period such as Arthur Schnitzler, Stefan Zweig, Egon Schiele, Gustav Klimt, Adolf Loos, Theodor Herzl, and even Leon Trotsky were regular coffee house patrons.

AUSTRIAN WINE AND BEER

Austria has a long winemaking tradition and produces both white and red varieties. Evidence of wine in urns in the area of Zagersdorf in Burgenland dates viticulture back to 700 B.C.

Austria has over 50,000 hectares of vineyard, almost all of it in the east or southeast of the country. Many of the approximately 20,000 small wine-producing estates base their finances on their direct retail of wine. Due to a decree that goes back to the so-called Maria Theresianische Buschenschankverordnung from 1784, a vintner can sell his own wine in his own house without any dedicated license to do so. The Grüner Veltliner is the dominant grape varietal cultivated in Austria, and the dry white wines produced from this grape have gained international recognition.

There are many different types of Austrian beer to be found. One of the most common brands of beer to be found in Austria is Stiegl, founded in 1492.

SPECIALTY DRINKS

Trying to fight his jetlag in East-Asia, the Austrian entrepreneur Dietrich Mateschitz learned about the Thai energy drink Krating Daeng. Adapting the idea for European markets, he founded the Red Bull Company in 1984. After massive growth in Austria, the brand was exported to Hungary, and soon in every corner of the world, selling billions of cans in about 130 countries. Hence Red Bull is the best-selling export of Austria. Next to the actual products, Red

Bull produces the company also concentrates on sports sponsorships, for instance, in soccer, skiing or sports flying.

ALMDUDLER

Since 1957, Almdudler has been one of the most popular fizzy soft drinks in Austria. Taking the expression "auf der Alm dudeln" (old Viennese dialect for "yodeling on the meadows") and the delicious flavors of Alpine meadowland herbs as his inspiration, Erwin Klein had struck upon a way of capturing and bottling the essence of the Austrian mountains. Today, Almdudler has established itself as Austria's national drink. The first beverage is a sweetened drink made out of a grape, and apple juice concentrates and is flavored with 32 natural herbs. To some extent, its taste can be compared to the taste of Ginger Ale but with a fruitier and sweeter flavor.

ELDERBERRY SYRUP

Elderberry syrup is ubiquitous in Austria. It is commonly made from an extract of elderflower blossoms and is used in various mixed drinks but also, for cooking and baking. You can even find Palatschinken (crêpes) with elderberry filling.

MOST

Most, from the Latin vinum mustum (young wine), is freshly pressed fruit juice. The most common kind is the one made from grapes, which is also the first step to making wine. This famous alcoholic drink is very common to Lower Austria, especially the regions between the Mostviertel ("must quarter") in the West of Vienna and the Bucklige Welt ("humpy world") in the Southeast. The Bucklige Welt is primarily known for its numerous "Most-Heurige" (from the Austrian "heurig" from this year), which are seasonal wine taverns, where this year's wine and a limited selection of food is served in an elementary and sociable setting. For the Bucklige Welt region, apple must be especially typical.

STURM

Sturm (storm, from the cloudy appearance) is a new wine that is in the process of fermentation (basically the steps between must and young wine). It is made of white or red grapes and, in contrast to most, it contains alcohol. According to the Austrian wine law, it is only allowed to be sold between August 1 and December 31 and must have an alcohol content of volume of at least 1 %.

SPRITZER

Spritzer (or G'spritzter, from the German word *spritzen*, i.e., spatter, squirt, spray, sprinkle) is a popular summer drink in Austria where it has developed to an integral part of its culture. This Austrian creation is traditionally made with white wine and soda or sparkling mineral water. It can be enjoyed as an aperitif, with a meal or only as a thirst quencher. To make a sweet version of the Spritzer, fresh lemonade like Sprite is added to the white wine instead of soda water. Sometimes red wine is used instead of white wine.
Aperol Spritz is a Spritzer mixed with Aperol and is served with a slice of orange. It is either an aperitif or a refreshing summer drink enjoyed by itself. Though originally from Italy, it has developed into a popular summer drink in Austria within the last couple of years.

Kaiserspritzer is a traditional variation of the Spritzer that adds elderberry syrup to the white wine and soda water. *Hugo-Spritzer* is a variation of the Kaiserspritzer, but it is not as sweet – fresh mint is added to white wine, soda water, and elderberry syrup.

RADLER

Especially enjoyed during the summer, the Radler is a beer-based mixed drink, which has a long-standing tradition in Austria. The Radler is usually mixed with either Almdudler, Sprite, or a lemon-based lemonade. During the summer months, Radler is very popular due to its reputation of being a thirst-quencher. Various breweries are now offering the product in bottles and cans.

Growing up around these dishes has shaped my culinary background and my desire to sample new foods and explore the rich history of its origin.

SOUPS

APFEL - SELLERIESUPPE

 FRITTATENSUPPE
(chicken soup with julienne crêpe)

Serves 4

FRITTATEN

3	eggs, beaten
1	cup flour – all purpose
1	cup milk
2	tablespoons butter melted
1.5	quarts consommé (chicken broth)
2	tablespoon sliced chives
	salt and pepper, to taste

HOW TO MAKE IT

1. In a mixing bowl, whisk together eggs, flour, and milk to make a smooth batter free of lumps, then season to taste with salt and pepper.
2. In 8-inch nonstick skillet, heat ½ tablespoon butter over medium-high heat.
3. Add ¼ of the batter, swirling the pan so a thin crêpe form. Cook until the bottom of the crêpe has browned, about 3 minutes, then flip and continue to cook until the other side has browned, about 2 more minutes.
4. Remove crêpe from pan and repeat with remaining butter and batter.
5. Roll up the crêpe and slice the crêpes into julienne / *joōlē'en/ (thin strips)*.
6. Heat the consommé *(broth)* and pour it into 4 bowls. Divide the sliced crêpes among the bowls and garnish with sliced chives.

LEBERKNÖDELSUPPE
(beef broth with liver dumplings)

Serves 4

LEBERKNÖDEL

½	pound ground pork liver	2	ounces butter (salted)
2	large eggs beaten	3	dinner rolls, softened in milk
2	tablespoons breadcrumb	1	medium onion finely chopped
1	each garlic clove chopped	2	ounces parsley chopped
2	quarts consommé (beef broth)	2	tablespoon sliced chives
	salt, pepper, marjoram to taste		

HOW TO MAKE IT

1. Heat ½ the butter in a pan, sauté the onion and garlic
2. Beat the rest of the butter with spices and eggs until it is foamy. Soak the rolls in milk first to soften them, press out the milk, and rip into small pieces. Mix with the ground pork liver, parsley, breadcrumbs, onion, and garlic and sauté for about 12-15 minutes.
3. Form the dumplings into golf-ball-size spheres. Place into consommé at a low boil and simmer for 15 minutes.
4. Heat the consommé *(beef broth)* and pour it into 4 bowls. Divide the leberknödel among the bowls and garnish with sliced chives.

GULASCHSUPPE
(hungarian style beef soup)

Serves 4

GULASCHSUPPE

1	pound stew beef	1	quart consommé (beef broth)
½	pound potatoes	½	cup red wine (optional)
3	tablespoon tomato puree (can)	½	cup red wine (optional)
2	medium white onions	½	cup clarified butter
1	each red pepper,	1	each bay leaves
1	each garlic cloves	1	tablespoon tomato paste
1	celery stalks sliced	2	tablespoon flour
1	medium carrot sliced	1	tablespoon lemon zest
3	tablespoons sweet hungarian paprika		salt & black pepper to taste

HOW TO MAKE IT

1. Cut beef into 1-inch pieces; chop onions and garlic cloves; wash and chop the soup greenery into smaller pieces.
2. Heat the clarified butter in a mid-size pot, add the onions and cook very slowly over low heat and stir until they are transparent.
3. Add carrot, celery, and beef. Keep cooking for 3-4 min.
4. Sprinkle flour over it; add tomato puree and red wine plus the consommé.
5. Let it boil on low heat for 1-2 hours or longer if needed (meat has to be tender)
6. Peel potato; cut them and the red pepper into small cubes.
7. Add potatoes, pepper, lemon zest, and bay leaves, cook for 15 more minutes.
8. If the soup is too thick add more broth; if the soup is too thin add more tomato puree.
9. Remove the bay leaves and Serve with a Kaiser rolls.

WIENER KARTOFFELSUPPE
(viennese potato soup)

Serves 4

KARTOFFELSUPPE

12	ounces potatoes diced	1	medium onion diced
6	ounce bacon diced	4	ounces carrots diced
4	ounces celery diced	3	ounces vegetable oil
6	ounces flour all-purpose	1	quart beef broth
1	teaspoon caraway seeds	1	each garlic clove chopped
1	tablespoon parsley chopped	1	each bay leaf
4	ounces mushroom	1	tablespoon rice vinegar
2	tablespoon sour cream	2	tablespoon fresh chive sliced
	salt & pepper to taste		

HOW TO MAKE IT

1. Sauté sliced mushrooms with 1 oz. of oil until tender.
2. Diced potatoes ½ inch.
3. Heat oil in a large soup pot; sauté the onion, bacon, carrots and celery slowly until translucent.
4. Add the flour, sauté lightly, add beef broth, and blend until smooth. Season with salt, pepper, caraway seed, chopped garlic, chopped parsley, and bay leaf.
5. Add sautéed mushrooms and cook for 15 more minutes, then add the diced potatoes and cook until they are soft.
6. Stir in the sour cream, remove from heat and season with salt, pepper, and vinegar.
7. Garnish with sliced chive!

BLUMENKOHLSUPPE
(cream of cauliflower soup)

Serves 4

BLUMENKOHLSUPPE

1	each head cauliflower, cleaned; chopped	1	cup celery chopped
3	each medium carrot, washed and sliced	2	each fresh garlic minced
2	stalks leeks, washed, dried, sliced	4	cups vegetable stock
2	cups spinach washed chopped	½	teaspoon cayenne
2	cups chard washed chopped	1	cup raw cashews chopped
2	teaspoon chopped parsley		sale & pepper to taste

HOW TO MAKE IT
You will LOVE this Vegetarian Soup

1. Heat the vegetable stock in a stockpot and bring to a boil.
2. Add chopped cauliflower, carrots, leeks, and garlic. Cover and simmer for about 10 minutes, add spinach and chard, and cook until the vegetables are tender.
3. Add all ingredients, including the broth into a food processor or blender, and blend until smooth and creamy.
4. To serve, add chopped cashews as décor, finish with a sprinkle of finely chopped parsley and serve hot.

APFEL - SELLERIESUPPE
(apple celery soup)

Serves 4

APFEL - SELLERIESUPPE

¼	cup butter	1.5	cups chopped vidalia onion
½	cup chopped chives	½	cup grapeseed oil
4	ounces thinly sliced bacon	4	cups chicken broth
4	cups ½ inch cubes peeled cleaned celery root		
3	cups ½ inch cubes peeled cored granny smith apples		
	salt & pepper to taste		

HOW TO MAKE IT

1. Melt butter in a large pot over medium heat.
2. Add celery root and chopped onion, cook until translucent.
3. Add apples, cook 15 more minutes, stirring often.
4. Add 3 cups of chicken broth, cover and bring to simmer.
5. Reduce heat to medium-low; simmer covered until celery root and apples are soft, occasionally stirring, about 5 minutes.
6. Remove from heat; cool slightly.
7. Puree soup in a blender until smooth, add more consommé to desired consistency.
8. Return soup to pot. Season to taste with salt and pepper and keep hot.
9. Puree chives, oil, and a pinch of salt in a blender until smooth.
10. In a medium sauté pan, cook sliced bacon until browned and crispy, about 6 minutes. Transfer to paper towels to drain.
11. Divide hot soup among bowls. Sprinkle crispy bacon on each serving. Drizzle each bowl with chive oil.

CHAMPIGNONCRÈME SUPPE
(cream of mushroom soup)

Serves 4

CHMPIGNONSUPPE

4	cups beef stock	3	ounces chopped onion
1	pound thinly sliced mushrooms	4	tablespoons butter
1	tablespoon oil	4	teaspoons dry sherry
2	ounces flour all-purpose	4	ounces heavy cream
1	tablespoon chopped chives or parsley (your preference)		
	salt & pepper to taste		

HOW TO MAKE IT

1. This is one of my favorite soups; *you can replace the beef broth with vegetarian broth to keep it vegetarian.*
2. In a medium sauté pan, heat oil; add chopped onion and cook until translucent sauté the sliced mushrooms until tender and browned.
3. In a soup pot, heat butter until melted; when melted, add the flour and sauté for 2-3 minutes until lightly brown.
4. Add the beef broth, sherry, and heavy cream and bring to a light boil. (have the soup smile and not laugh)
5. Simmer broth for 2-3 minutes. Add sautéed mushroom and cook for an additional 2 minutes.
6. Ladle soup in a bowl and sprinkle with chopped chive or parsley.

KÜRBISCREMESUPPE

(cream of pumpkin soup)

Serves 4

KÜRBISCREMESUPPE

3	oz salted butter	1	large onion finely chopped
2	garlic cloves finely chopped	½	cup of dry white wine
3	cup of vegetable broth	2	cans of pumpkin puree
½	cup of Heavy Cream		salt and pepper to taste
4	teaspoons toasted pumpkin seeds	2	teaspoon pumpkin seed oil (optional)
1	teaspoon grated nutmeg		
1	tablespoon oil		

HOW TO MAKE IT

1. In a medium soup pot melt butter. Add oil;
2. Add the chopped onion and garlic and cook until they become translucent.
3. Add the white wine and vegetable broth and let it come to a soft boil.
4. Add pumpkin puree and stir to incorporate it completely. Reduce the heat down to low.
5. Puree soup with an immersion blender until it's nice and smooth.
6. Add in the cream and stir well. The soup should be a bold yellow orange in color.
7. Let it heat through for about 5 stirring frequently.
8. Season to taste with salt pepper and ground nutmeg.
9. To serve pour soup into a bowl and garnish roasted pumpkin seeds and a drizzle of pumpkin seed oil. You can replace the pumpkin seed oil with balsamic vinegar if desired.

 GRIESSNOCKERLSUPPE
(semolina dumpling soup)

Serves 4

NOCKERL

1	large egg
½	teaspoon salt
2	tablespoon butter
5	tablespoon semolina
½	teaspoon nutmeg grated

SOUP

4	cups chicken broth
4	oz sliced carrots
3	oz sliced and cleaned celery
1	medium onion chopped
2	oz thinly sliced chive
2	oz oil
2	garlic cloves minced

HOW TO MAKE IT

1. In a soup medium soup pot heat oil on medium heat.
2. Add chopped onion; cook for 3 min and add minced garlic, cook until onion is translucent.
3. Add celery and Carrots and keep cooking for 3 min.
4. Add chicken stock and bring to a light boil; cook for 15 min.
5. In a small mixing bowl, whip room temperature butter until it is creamy.
6. Add beaten egg, salt, nutmeg, and semolina. Mix until all ingredients are incorporated. Cover and let the mixture rest 15-20 min. in the refrigerator.
7. Dip two soup spoons into the water and form the dumplings (Nockerln). With one spoon, take the dough out of the bowl, with the second you bring the dumpling to its form.
8. Add formed dumplings into light boiling soup and cook until the dumpling rises.
9. Serve dumplings with broth and vegetables and top with fresh chive.

 WIENER ZWIEBELSUPPE
(viennese onion soup)

Serves 4

ZWIEBELSUPPE

1	medium yellow onion	1	medium red onion
1	medium leek (white portion only)	5	green onions with tops
1	garlic clove, minced	2	tablespoons butter
2	cans (14-1/2 ounces each) beef broth	4	oz beef consommé, undiluted
1	teaspoon Worcestershire sauce	½	teaspoon ground nutmeg
1	cup shredded Swiss cheese		
4	slices French bread (3/4 inch thick), toasted		
4	tablespoons grated Parmesan cheese, optional		

HOW TO MAKE IT

1. Slice all onions and leeks into ¼ inch thick pieces.
2. In a large saucepan, sauté onions and garlic over medium heat for 10 min or until tender and golden. Stirring occasionally.
3. Add broth, consommé, Worcestershire sauce, and ground nutmeg.
4. Bring to a boil, reduce heat, cover and simmer for about 30 minutes.
5. Sprinkle 1 tablespoon of shredded swiss cheese in the bottom of six ovenproof 8-oz—soup bowls.
6. Ladle hot soup into bowls. Top each with toasted slices of bread.
7. Sprinkle remaining swiss cheese and parmesan cheese if desired.
8. Broil 6-8 minutes with top heat or until cheese is melted and has the desired golden color.
9. Serve Immediately.

 KNOBLAUCHCRÈMESUPPE
(creamy garlic soup with croûtons)

Serves 4

KNOBLAUCHSUPPE

8	garlic cloves (coarsely chopped)
5	pieces of bread (diced)
1	qt. vegetable stock
2	cups heavy cream
1	teaspoon parsley cleaned and chopped
½	teaspoon white pepper
½	teaspoon salt
4	tablespoons grated Parmesan cheese, optional

CROÛTONS

4	slices of bread (diced)
2	tablespoons olive oil
1	tablespoons butter
1	garlic clove (finely chopped)

HOW TO MAKE IT

1. Peel garlic cloves and chop coarsely. Cut the toast into chunky cubes.
2. In a stockpot, bring vegetable stock and cream to the boil, add garlic, salt and simmer for 5 minutes.
3. Add the bread cubes and simmer for a further 10 minutes.
4. In the meantime, slice the croûton bread into small cubes for the croûtons.
5. Heat olive oil and butter in a sauté pan and add the crushed garlic. Add the bread cubes and fry until crispy on the outside. Do not leave unattended for too long to ensure nothing is burnt and then put them to one side.
6. Purée the cream soup and garnish with chopped parsley.
7. Finish with parmesan cheese (optional).

RINDSSUPPE
(classic austrian beef soup)

Serves 4

RINDSSUPPE

3	qt. cold water	4	ounces celery
1	pound stew beef	4	ounces parsley roots
1	medium onion (peeled)	2	tablespoon clarified butter
4	ounces peeled carrots	½	teaspoon white pepper
4	ounces yellow beets	1	tablespoon salt
1	tablespoon chopped parsley or green onions		

HOW TO MAKE IT

1. Wash the soup meat very well with warm water. Place in cold water and bring to a boil. Use a ladle to skim off any foam that may rise. Please have the broth smile and not lough.
2. Clean the root vegetables, peel, and chop them as you like, cut the onion in half (with the bowl, the soup gets a darker color. You can also roast them briefly in a pan (it is better for the taste) and add to the meat stock (Beef should be boiling for about an hour), add the spices, let the soup boil gently so that it does not become cloudy.
3. Total cooking time: approx. 2½ hours
4. Strain and taste the soup, serve with the root vegetables, and shredded beef. Finish with chopped parsley or green onions.

ROTKOHLSALAT MIT GRÜNEM APFEL UND GERÖSTETEN WALNÜSSEN

SALADS

WARMER ERDÄPFELSALAT

RÜBENSALAT MIT APFEL

GRÜNER SALAT MIT FRESCHEN BIRNEN

 WARMER ERDÄPFELSALAT
(warm austrian potato salad)

Serves 4

WARMER ERDÄPFELSALAT

1	pound fingerling potatoes washed
4	ounces chicken consommé
2.5	tablespoon salt
1	cup vinegar (white)
1	teaspoon pepper black
2	tablespoon chopped chives or parsley
1	cup chopped red onion
4	tablespoons oil
3	teaspoons sugar
2	tablespoon mustard whole grain

HOW TO MAKE IT

1. In a large saucepan, combine the potatoes and 2 tablespoons of the salt. Add enough cold water to cover completely.
2. Bring to a boil over high heat. Reduce the heat to maintain a simmer and cook until the potatoes are just tender enough to be pierced easily with a fork, about 10 minutes.
3. Drain the potatoes. While they are still hot, peel them with a small, sharp knife, protecting your hand from the heat with a folded kitchen towel. Cut the peeled potato into 1/4-inch slices while hot.
4. Place sliced potatoes into a medium mixing bowl; add sliced onion, remaining salt, mustard, sugar, pepper, vinegar, and oil. Stir gently but thoroughly with a large spoon to combine all ingredients.
5. In a small pot, bring the chicken consommé to a boil and pour over the potato salad mix well and garnish with chive or parsley. Serve warm or cold!

GURKENSALAT
(cucumber salad)

Serves 4

GURKENSALAT

2	pound seedless cucumbers	1	tablespoon salt
¼	teaspoon pepper black	½	cup white-wine vinegar
¼	cup cold water	3	teaspoons sugar
1	teaspoon mustard	1	teaspoon sugar
1	each garlic clove, minced	1	teaspoon fresh dill

HOW TO MAKE IT

1. Cut cucumbers lengthwise with a knife and slice thin (if it is easier for you then can slice it with a disk of a food processor.
2. In a large bowl, toss cucumber with salt and let stand 1 hour.
3. Keep them cold.
4. In a small saucepan, bring vinegar and water to a boil with sugar, garlic, mustard, and dill, stirring until sugar is dissolved.
5. Let dressing cool.
6. In a strainer drain cucumbers and rinse under cold water. Drain cucumbers well, squeezing out excess liquid. In a bowl, combine cucumber with dressing and let it marinate, covered and chilled, for about an hour.
7. Toss with fresh dill.
8. Serve chilled.

TOMATENSALAT
(tyrolian tomato salad)

Serves 4

TOMATENSALAD
2	pound plum tomatoes	1	teaspoon salt
1	each medium red onion sliced	2	tablespoon basil chopped
1	teaspoon Austrian pumpkin seed oil		

VINAIGRETTE
(makes about ½ cup)

2	tablespoons finely chopped shallots	2	tablespoons red- or white-wine vinegar
¼	teaspoon fine sea salt, or to taste	6	tablespoons extra-virgin olive oil
2	teaspoons Dijon mustard		
	Freshly ground black pepper to taste		

HOW TO MAKE IT

1. VINAIGRETTE: In a small bowl, whisk together the shallots, vinegar, and sea salt; let the mixture stand 10 minutes. Whisk in the mustard, then add the oil in very slowly, thin, steady stream, constantly whisking until the dressing is emulsified. Season with fine sea salt and freshly ground black pepper.
2. DO AHEAD: *The vinaigrette can be prepared ahead and refrigerated, in an airtight container, up to a week.*
3. SALAD: Wash and slice the tomatoes into slices.
4. Slice cleaned red onion into thin slices; Chop washed, cleaned basil
5. In a bowl place sliced tomatoes, add sliced red onion, add chopped basil, add chilled vinaigrette
6. Serve chilled and drizzle with the roasted Austrian pumpkin seed oil.

 WARMER KRAUTSALAT
(warm cabbage salad)

Serves 4

KRAUTSALAT

¼	cup dried currants or raisins	3	tablespoons balsamic vinegar
6	cups thinly sliced red cabbage	4	ounce thinly sliced bacon
2	tablespoon finely chopped shallot	2	tablespoon extra-virgin olive oil
½	cup walnuts coarsely chopped		
¼	cup chopped fresh Italian parsley	1	each fresh pear thinly sliced
	salt & pepper to taste		

HOW TO MAKE IT

1. Place currants in a small mixing bowl. Heat balsamic vinegar in a saucepan over medium heat until hot (do not boil). Pour vinegar over currants; let soak until currants soften, 15 to 20 minutes.
2. Place cabbage in a large mixing bowl; set aside. Heat large sauté pan over medium-high heat.
3. Add sliced bacon; sauté until brown and crisp, about 5 minutes. Add shallot to bacon keep sautéing for another minute.
4. Remove from heat. Stir in currant- vinegar mixture and olive oil. Season with salt and freshly ground black pepper.
5. Add sliced pears to cabbage and toss.
6. Pour bacon mixture over cabbage-pear mixture and toss to coat. Season to taste with salt and pepper. Let the mixture rest for 5 minutes.
7. Add chopped walnuts and parsley; toss to blend. Serve warm.

# GRÜNER BOHNENSALAT
(green bean salad)

Serves 4

BOHNENSALAT

1	pound green beans, ends trimmed	1	tablespoons olive oil
1	cup medium diced swiss cheese	2	tablespoons balsamic vinegar
1	cup cherry tomatoes, sliced in half		
4	tablespoons chopped red onion	2	tablespoons chopped fresh chive
1	large clove garlic, minced		
	salt & pepper to taste		

HOW TO MAKE IT

1. In a large stockpot, bring saltwater to a boil.
2. Add green beans and cook until tender-crisp 1-2 minutes.
3. Use a strainer to remove crisp green beans to a bowl of ice water.
4. Chill quickly and drain well.
5. In a large mixing bowl, combine green beans, diced swiss cheese, sliced tomatoes, and red onions.
6. Whisk together the olive oil, balsamic vinegar, pumpkin seed oil, chive and garlic.
7. Pour the dressing over green bean mixture; toss and add salt and pepper taste.
8. Let marinate in the refrigerator for 1-12 hours.
9. Serve cold.

 # SPARGELSALAT MIT WACHTELEIER
(asparagus salad with quail eggs)

Serves 4

SPAGELSALAT

8	each quail eggs	1	pound green asparagus trimmed
1	tablespoon white-wine vinegar		
1	tablespoon champagne vinegar	2	teaspoons whole grain mustard
1/3	cup grapeseed oil		
1	small shallot, thinly sliced into rings	3	teaspoons chopped fresh tarragon
1	cup baby spinach leaves		
½	teaspoon red pepper flakes		salt & pepper to taste

HOW TO MAKE IT

1. In a small stockpot, cover eggs with cold water. Bring to a simmer and cook, covered, 5 minutes. Rinse eggs under cold running water to stop cooking, then peel and quarter. Keep chilled.
2. Cut asparagus on a bias into 3/4-inch-thick slices, leaving tips.
3. In a medium pot boil asparagus tip for 1-2 minutes, then transfer to a bowl of ice water to stop cooking. Drain well and pat dry with paper towels.
4. Whisk together vinegar and mustard.
5. Add oil in a slow stream, whisking, add red pepper flakes and stir in shallot.
6. Add tarragon, and salt and pepper to taste.
7. Toss asparagus and clean baby spinach with vinaigrette and place on 4 plates.
8. Tuck quail eggs decoratively into salads. Serve cold.

 GRÜNER SALAT MIT FRESCHEN BIRNEN
(field greens salad with fresh pears)

Serves 4

BIRNENSALAT

6	cups salad greens	2	pears, peeled and sliced
⅓	cup walnuts, coarsely chopped		

VINAIGRETTE
(makes about ½ cup)

2	tablespoons finely chopped shallots	2	tablespoons red- or white-wine vinegar
¼	teaspoon fine sea salt, or to taste		
2	teaspoons Dijon mustard	6	tablespoons extra-virgin olive oil
	Freshly ground black pepper to taste		

HOW TO MAKE IT

1. Prepare the vinaigrette by mixing together all ingredients and chill.
2. Toss the vinaigrette with the salad greens.
3. Top with the fresh pears and chopped walnut.
4. Serve chilled.

EVDIVIESALAT MIT APFEL
(endive salad with fresh apples)

Serves 4

ENDIVIESALAT

¼	cup olive oil	2	tablespoons apple cider vinegar
1	tablespoon orange juice	1	teaspoon honey
¼	cup pecans	2	heads of endive, chopped
1	cup arugula	1	apple, sliced thin
¼	cup dried cherries	¼	cup of camembert cheese
	Salt and pepper to taste		

HOW TO MAKE IT

1. To make the dressing: In a small bowl, whisk together the oil, vinegar, juice, and honey. Season with salt and pepper.
2. In a small sauté pan, toast the pecans over medium heat. Allow cooling.
3. Mix together the endive, arugula, apple, and cherries in a medium-size bowl. Toss with enough dressing to coat. Top with the pecans and camembert cheese.

 TOMATENSALAT MIT AVOCADO
(tomato - avocado salad)

Serves 4

TOMATENSALAT

1	pound roma tomatoes	2	tablespoon extra-virgin olive oil
1	each english cucumber	2	tablespoon fresh lemon juice
½	medium red onion sliced	¼	cup chopped cilantro
2	fresh ripe avocados diced	¼	teaspoon black pepper
1	teaspoon sea salt	½	teaspoon whole grain mustard
1	tablespoon balsamic vinegar	½	tablespoon water

HOW TO MAKE IT

1. Cut the cleaned fresh tomatoes, cucumbers and avocado into a small piece.
2. Clean red onion and slice into julienne.
3. In a small mixing bowl, add the salt, pepper, vinegar, lemon juice, oil, mustard, and water. Mix well.
4. Add the chopped onion, tomato, cucumber, avocado, and cilantro and gently stir. (if you don't like cilantro you can replace it with fresh basil on parsley)
5. Serve cold!

MELONENSALAT MIT PROSCIUTTO
(cantaloupe salad with prosciutto and austrian ice wine dressing)

Serves 4

MELONENSALAT

8	sliced of prosciutto	2	cups baby mache
1	ripe cantaloupe		(or butter lettuce)

VINAIGRETTE

½	tablespoons finely chopped shallots	½	cup ice-wine
1	tablespoon extra-virgin olive oil	½	teaspoon pepper
1	tablespoon champagne vinegar	¼	teaspoon fine sea salt
½	tablespoon balsamic vinegar		

HOW TO MAKE IT

1. In a small bowl, stir together the wine, olive oil, Champagne vinegar, shallots and balsamic vinegar and season with salt and pepper.
2. Drizzle 1 1/2 tablespoons of the dressing over the cantaloupe slices and turn the slices to coat evenly. (At this point, the dish may be covered and refrigerated for no more than 1 hour before continuing.)
3. Divide the cantaloupe slices evenly among individual serving plates. Drape 2 prosciutto slice over the cantaloupe slices on each plate.
4. Put the mache leaves in the shallow dish you used for dressing the cantaloupe slices, add the remaining dressing, and toss until the leaves are evenly coated.
5. Arrange the mache attractively on each plate, dividing it evenly. Serve immediately.

RÜBENSALAT MIT APFEL
(red beet salad with fresh apples)

Serves 4

RÜBENSALAT

4	large red or yellow beets	2	thyme sprig
2	fuji apples		

VINAIGRETTE

1	tablespoon finely chopped shallots	¼	cup apple cider vinegar
¼	cup extra-virgin olive oil	½	teaspoon mustard
2	tablespoon fresh horseradish (use jarred horseradish if needed)	1	tablespoon pistachios
		¼	teaspoon black pepper
½	tablespoon balsamic vinegar	¼	teaspoon fine sea salt

HOW TO MAKE IT

1. Preheat the oven to 375°. In a baking dish, lightly drizzle the beets and thyme with olive oil. Season with salt and pepper.
2. Cover with foil and roast until the beets are tender, about 1 hour and 45 minutes.
3. Let cool, then peel the beets and cut them into 3/4-inch dice.
4. In a large bowl, whisk the vinegar, shallots with the mustard.
5. Whisk in the remaining 1/2 cup of oil until emulsified.
6. Add the horseradish and season with salt and pepper; toss with the beets and pistachios.
7. Transfer the beets to a platter, top with the apple and serve.

RETTICHSALAT MIT KÜRBISKERNEN UND KÜRBISÖL
(radish salad with pumpkin seeds and pumpkin seed oil)

Serves 4

RETTICHSALAT

½	pound sliced radishes	½	tablespoon chives
½	tablespoon chopped parsley	2	cups mixed salad greens
1	tablespoon pumpkin seed oil	¼	cup raw pumpkin seeds

VINAIGRETTE

2	tablespoon extra-virgin olive oil	½	teaspoon pepper
2	tablespoon champagne vinegar	¼	teaspoon fine sea salt
½	tablespoon rice vinegar	½	teaspoon sugar
½	teaspoon whole grain mustard		

HOW TO MAKE IT

1. Preheat the oven to 375°. Spread the pumpkin seeds in a pie plate and toast for about 5 minutes, until lightly golden.
2. Transfer the seeds to a small bowl; add 1/4 teaspoon of the canola oil, season with salt, and toss.
3. Meanwhile, in a small bowl, whisk the rice vinegar, champagne vinegar, mustard, and sugar with the remaining olive oil and season the vinaigrette with salt and pepper.
4. In a medium bowl, toss the radishes with 2 tablespoons of the vinaigrette. Arrange the radishes on plates or a platter.
5. Sprinkle the herbs and the toasted pumpkin seeds on top and drizzle with the pumpkin seed oil. Toss the microgreens with the remaining vinaigrette.
6. Top the radish salad with the microgreens and serve.

ROTKOHLSALAT MIT GRÜNEM APFEL UND GERÖSTETEN WALNÜSSEN
(red cabbage salad with green apple, and toasted walnuts)

Serves 8

ROTKOHLSALAT

3	tablespoons lingonberry jam	1	tablespoons Dijon mustard
1	tablespoon red wine vinegar	½	cup olive oil
2	red apples, grated	½	cup walnut halves
4	cups sliced red cabbage	½	teaspoon nutmeg

HOW TO MAKE IT

1. Puree 1 tablespoon preserves, mustard, nutmeg, and vinegar in a blender.
2. Gradually add oil. Season dressing to taste with salt and pepper.
3. Reserve 1/4 of grated apple and several walnut halves for garnish.
4. Toss cabbage, remaining 2 tablespoons preserves, apple, and walnuts in a large bowl. Toss with enough dressing to coat.
5. Season to taste with salt and pepper.
6. Garnish with reserved grated apple and walnut halves and serve.

 FRISCHER GEMÜSESALAT
(summer chop salad)

Serves 4

GEMÜSESALAT

1	cup diced carrots	¾	cup fresh corn kernels
½	cup diced green beans	½	cup diced red onion
½	cup diced radicchio	½	cup diced celery
1	vine-ripened tomato diced	4	teaspoon grated Parmesan
2	cups mixed baby salad leaves, reserve a few small leaves for garnish		
8	cherry tomatoes, halved	½	tablespoon Dijon mustard
1 ½	tablespoon balsamic vinegar	1	tablespoon sherry vinegar
3	tablespoon olive oil	1	tablespoon safflower oil
	Kosher salt and black pepper for taste		

HOW TO MAKE IT

1. For the Dijon-Balsamic Vinaigrette: In a bowl, whisk together the mustard, balsamic vinegar, and sherry vinegar. Whisking continuously, slowly drizzle in the oils to form a smooth emulsion. Season to taste with salt and pepper. Use immediately or cover and refrigerate for up to 1 week.
2. Bring a pot of salted water to a boil. Fill a bowl with ice cubes and water. Put the carrots, corn, and green beans in a wire sieve, lower it into the boiling water, and cook until the vegetables are tender-crisp, 2 to 3 minutes. Plunge the sieve into the ice water to stop the cooking process. Drain well.
3. In a large bowl, combine the blanched vegetables, onion, radicchio, celery, and tomato. Put the salad leaves in a separate bowl.
4. Drizzle about two-thirds of the vinaigrette over the chopped vegetable mixture and toss well. Sprinkle in the Parmesan. Season to taste with salt and pepper. Drizzle the remaining dressing over the salad leaves and toss well.
5. Arrange beds of salad leaves on four chilled salad plates. Mound the chopped vegetable salad on top. Top the vegetables with the reserved salad leaves. Arrange cherry tomato halves around the base of the mixture. Serve immediately.

FRISCHER GEMÜSESALAT

SIDE DISHES

KRAUTSTRUDEL

HABSBURGER SCHWAMMERLGULASCH

AUSTRIAN SPÄTZLE MIT KÄSE UND KARAMELLIERTEN ZWIEBELN

AUSTRIAN SPÄTZLE MIT KÄSE UND KARAMELLIERTEN ZWIEBELN

(austrian pasta with cheese and caramelized onions)

Serves 6

SPÄTZLE

1 ¾	cup milk	¼	teaspoon freshly grated nutmeg
4	large egg yolks	1	large egg
2	tablespoon oil	1	tablespoon unsalted butter
5	ounces shredded gruyere	3	cups all-purpose flour
1	large white onion, sliced		salt and pepper to taste

HOW TO MAKE IT

1. In a small bowl, whisk together the milk, egg yolks, and egg. In a large bowl, whisk together the flour with the nutmeg, 1 teaspoon of salt, and 1/4 teaspoon of pepper. With a wooden spoon, stir the egg mixture into the flour mixture just until blended but still slightly lumpy. Cover the bowl with plastic wrap and refrigerate the batter for at least 1 hour or as long as overnight.
2. Bring a large pot of salted water to a boil. Prepare a large bowl of ice water. Carefully hold a colander with large holes over the boiling water. Add about 1/2 cup of the batter to the strainer and, with a rubber spatula or the back of a large spoon, press the mixture through the holes to drop into the simmering water. Repeat until all of the batter has been used.
3. Cook for 2 minutes, then drain thoroughly. Immediately transfer the spätzle to the ice water, stirring until all of the ice has melted. Drain the spätzle and transfer them to a large bowl. Stir in 1 tablespoon of the oil, season lightly with salt and pepper, and toss to coat. Set aside. (You can prepare the recipe to this point up to a day ahead and refrigerate the spätzle.)

CONTINUED

1. Preheat the oven to 400 degrees F. Oil a 9-by-13-inch baking dish. Spread the spätzle evenly in the dish and dot with the butter pieces. Sprinkle evenly with the cheese and bake until the spätzle are hot, and the cheese is melted about 20 minutes.
2. As soon as you put the spätzle in the oven, heat the remaining 1 tablespoon oil in a medium skillet over high heat. Add the onion and cook, stirring, until softened slightly, about 1 minute. Reduce the heat to medium-low and cook, occasionally stirring until the onions are lightly browned, about 15 minutes. As soon as the spätzle are ready, scatter the onions over them and serve immediately.

TIRLOER GRÖSTL
(traditional tyrolian hash)

Serves 4

GRÖSTL

1	pound boiled, cooled potatoes	6	ounces bacon chopped
6	ounces cooked beef	1	cup chopped onions
2	tablespoon butter	4	eggs
1	tablespoon olive oil	1	tablespoon chopped chive
	Salt and pepper to taste		caraway seeds to taste

HOW TO MAKE IT

1. In a large skillet, melt the butter and sauté the finely chopped onion until golden brown. Add the diced bacon and beef and continue to sauté.
2. Cut the potatoes into slices and add to the pan.
3. Continue browning until heated through and crispy, stirring or flipping as needed. Season with salt and a pinch or two of caraway seeds.
4. In another pan, fry four eggs in olive oil.
5. Serve the "Tiroler Gröstl" with fried eggs on top, sprinkled with finely chopped chives.

 HABSBURGER SCHWAMMERLGULASCH
(habsburger mushroom goulash)

Serves 4

SCHWAMMERLGULASCH

8	ounces mushroom (your choice)	2	ounces chopped carrots
2	ounces chopped celery	4	ounces new potatoes
4	ounces spring onions	3	tablespoon butter
2	ounces chopped shallots	1	tablespoon sweet paprika
1	bay leaf	¼	teaspoon caraway seeds
5	ounces white wine	4	cups chicken stock
4	ounces sour cream	½	teaspoon fresh dill
3	tablespoon apple juice	½	teaspoon salt
½	teaspoon pepper		balsamic vinegar to taste

HOW TO MAKE IT

1. Clean mushrooms with a moist sponge (if possible, don't wash). Cut into bite-size pieces. Cut carrots, celeriac, peeled potatoes and, spring onions into small cubes. Chop shallots finely.
2. Heat butter in a pot and sauté the shallots.
3. Add paprika powder, pour over white wine and, add all the vegetables (without the mushrooms) as well as the potatoes. Pour in the stock, add salt, pepper and the bay leaf. Boil for 10-15 minutes on high until the broth is thick.
4. Add mushrooms and simmer for another 5 minutes.
5. Remove the bay leaf.
6. Mix the sour cream with some hot stock or water.
7. Add the dill and lovage to the goulash.
8. Let simmer for a few more minutes, then add vinegar to taste.
9. Serve Hot.

 WIENER GEDÜNSTESTER ROTKOHL
(viennese stewed red cabbage)

Serves 4

GEDÜNSTETER ROTKOHL

1	large red cabbage	1	white onion finely chopped
2	tablespoon butter	2	tablespoon brown sugar
3	tablespoon olive oil	1	cup apple sliced
3	tablespoon red vinegar	2	ounces red wine
2	ounces vegetable stock	1	tablespoon flour all-purpose
3	tablespoon crème fraiche (or sour cream)		

HOW TO MAKE IT

1. Cut the cabbage into quarters, discard the outer leaves, cut away the hard-central core and shred each quarter finely.
2. In a large, deep pan melt the butter and oil over a moderate flame and add onions.
3. Sauté until the onions are translucent and just starting to color.
4. Add sugar to the onion and stir. Add cabbage to the pan and stir well.
5. Quarter the apple, chop it into little chunks and add to the pan, stir again.
6. Add vinegar to the pan, stir, season with salt and freshly ground black pepper, stir and cover. Cook over the moderate flame for 15 minutes.
7. After 15 mins add water, red wine and put the pan in the oven for 2 hours.
8. Remove the pan from the oven and cook on the stovetop over low flame.
9. Stir the flour into the creme fraiche or sour cream to make a paste; you are going to add this to the cabbage to thicken it slightly. Add a spoonful of the paste to the pan, keep stirring and then add another spoonful, stir and add the final spoonful for about 5 mins.
10. Remove from the heat, taste to see if you need to add more sugar or vinegar.
11. Serve hot!

KRAUTSTRUDEL
(cabbage strudel)

Serves 4

KRAUTSTRUDEL

5	ounces flour all-purpose	2.5	ounces warm water
1	teaspoon vinegar	a	pinch of salt
	flour for work surface	2	tablespoon butter for baking

FILLING

1	white onion diced	6	ounces bacon chopped
1	tablespoon white sugar	2	pound cabbage shredded
	salt and pepper to taste	½	teaspoon caraway seeds
	nutmeg to taste	¾	vegetable or chicken stock
1	egg		

HOW TO MAKE IT

1. In a medium mixing bowl; mix all ingredients together for the dough and knead to form a smooth dough which doesn't stick to the walls of the bowl. Shape the dough into a ball and brush with oil. To ensure it is easy to stretch, cover and leave to rest for approx. 30 minutes.
2. On a floured work surface roll out the dough as thin as you can; so, you can almost see through it.
3. In a medium stock pot cook the bacon until almost crisp, add sugar and caramelize it. Peel and finely chop the onions, add to the bacon and keep sautéing.
4. Add the shredded cabbage, deglaze with stock, season with salt, pepper and caraway. Cook until the cabbage is soft. Let the mixture cool for a few minutes.
5. Strain the liquid and spread the mixture on the side closed to you over the strudel dough. Roll the Cabbage Strudel, place on a buttered backing sheet. and bake for approx. 30 minutes until golden brown. Brush the strudel with egg wash To serve slice a two-finger big section as a side dish or as a meal with a salad.

EIERNUDELN MIT GERÖSTETEN SCHWAMMERLN

(noodles with roasted mushrooms)

Serves 4

EIERNUDELN

.5	pound wide egg noodles	5	ounces mushrooms chopped
3	tablespoon butter	1	shallot, chopped fine
1	small red onion chopped	4	tablespoon chopped chive
3	ounces shitake mushroom chopped	2	ounces vegetable stock
	Salt and pepper to taste	1	tablespoon virgin olive oil

HOW TO MAKE IT

1. Cook egg noodles until just tender in boiling salted water, about 8 minutes.
2. In a medium sauté pan, sauté red onions and shallots for about 3 mins with 1 tablespoon of butter over medium heat.
3. Add remaining butter and all mushrooms and shallot in 2 tablespoons butter and continue to sauté until mushrooms are tender about 3 or 4 minutes.
4. Deglaze with vegetable stock and bring to a boil.
5. Drain noodles and toss in with cooked mushrooms. Add the chives and season with a little salt, to taste.
6. Serve hot!

ÖSTERREICHISCHER WEISSER SPARGEL MIT BRAUNER BUTTER
(austrian white asparagus with brown butter sauce)

Serves 4

SPARGEL

12	white asparagus, peeled	4	ounces butter
1	cup brioche crumbs	1	teaspoon chopped parsley
	Salt and pepper to taste		

HOW TO MAKE IT

1. Peel the asparagus. Line the asparagus from the spear end and cut into approximately 6-inch lengths. Discard all ends.
2. In a medium saucepan, bring salted water to a boil.
3. Cook the asparagus for 12 minutes, until tender being careful not to overcook.
4. Drain the asparagus. Set aside. In a large sauté pan, heat the butter.
5. Add the brioche crumbs and sauté until golden.
6. Add the reserved asparagus and sauté until well coated with the browned butter and brioche crumbs. Sprinkle with parsley, season with salt and pepper.
7. Serve warm.

 STEIRISCHE SPÄTZLE
(styrian spätzle with parsley and butter)

Serves 4

SPÄTZLE

1	cup all-purpose flour	1	teaspoon salt
½	teaspoon black pepper	½	teaspoon ground nutmeg
2	large eggs	¼	cup milk
3	tablespoon salted butter	1	tablespoon chopped chives
	Salt and pepper to taste		

HOW TO MAKE IT

1. In a large bowl, combine the flour, salt, pepper, and nutmeg. In another mixing bowl, whisk the eggs and milk together.
2. Make a well in the center of the dry ingredients and pour in the egg-milk mixture.
3. Gradually draw in the flour from the sides and combine well; the dough should be smooth and thick. Let the dough rest for 10 to 15 minutes.
4. Bring 3 quarts of salted water to a boil in a large pot, then reduce to a simmer. To form the spätzle, hold a large-holed colander or slotted spoon over the simmering water and push the dough through the holes with a spatula or spoon. Do this in batches, so you don't overcrowd the pot. Cook for 3 to 4 minutes or until the spätzle floats to the surface, stirring gently to prevent sticking. Dump the spätzle into a colander and give it a quick rinse with cold water.
5. In a medium sauté pan, melt the butter over medium heat and add the spätzle, tossing to coat. Cook the spätzle for 1 to 2 minutes to give the noodles some color, and then sprinkle with the chopped chives and season with salt and pepper before serving.
6. Serve warm.

CHAMPIGNON UND PILZ RISOTTO
(wild mushroom risotto)

Serves 4

RISOTTO

½	cup olive oil	½	pound onion minced
1	each garlic clove minced	2	cups arborio rice
1	cup dry white wine	2	cups mushroom stock
5	cups chicken stock	3	tablespoon olive oil
½	pound wild mushrooms reserve stems for stock	2	ounces grated parmesan
	pinch chopped parsley	¼	cup tomato chopped, seeded
			salt and pepper to taste

HOW TO MAKE IT

1. In a medium-size heavy saucepan, heat the oil. Over medium-high heat, sauté the onion and garlic just to soften, stirring all the while, 3 to 4 minutes. Add the rice and continue to stir, using a wooden spoon, coating the rice with the oil and onion.
2. In a medium-size saucepan, heat the peanut oil. Over medium-high heat, sauté onion and garlic, stir, 3 to 4 minutes. Add rice and continue to stir, using a wooden spoon, coat the rice with the oil and onion.
3. Meanwhile, in a medium skillet, heat the olive oil. If the mushrooms are large, cut them into bite-size pieces and sauté over medium heat to soften.
4. Pour 3 cups of stock into the rice, turn the flame to high, and stir in a large pinch of salt and the tomatoes. Stir until almost al dente. Stir in the mushrooms and the remaining 1-cup of stock, as necessary. Remember that the risotto should be creamy, not runny. Remove from the flame and vigorously beat in the chilled butter and 1/2 cup of the Parmesan until completely dissolved. Stir in the parsley and season with salt and pepper to taste. Serve immediately.

ESTERHAZY ROSTBRATEN

ENTRÉE

WIENER SCHNITZEL

ÖSTERREICHISCHER TAFELSPITZ

TIROLER GEBRATENES HUHN

ÖSTERREICHISCHER TAFELSPITZ
(austrian boiled beef)

Serves 4

TAFELSPITZ

2	pound beef (bottom round)	1	pound beef bones
3	medium carrots	3	celery stalks
1	parsnip	1	turnip
½	leek stalk	5	garlic cloves
2	onions	2	tablespoon salt
1	tablespoon pepper	3	bay leaves
1	chili pepper hot	2	carrots for garnish
2	ounces chive		Salt and pepper to taste

HOW TO MAKE IT

1. Place the bones in a pot and pour them with hot water. Strain the liquid and rinse the bones in a sieve with warm water to remove bone fragments and clean the bones.
2. Add bones to a large pot. Bring to boil with 4-5 qt of cold water, the soup vegetables, and all the spices. Don't add salt yet.
3. Meanwhile, halve the onions and roast in a pan until dark brown. Add to soup. Add the "burnt" onion with their peels. This improves the taste and makes a beautiful brown color.
4. When the water boils, lightly salt, and add the Tafelspitz meat to the boiling soup, it should be fully covered with the liquid.
5. After about 1 hour of cooking, remove vegetables, onions, and garlic, so the soup does not become too sweet. Simmer for about 3 hours on low heat.
6. Sieve the meat and serve the soup before the main dish. About 15 minutes before serving, add small pieces of carrots to the soup.
7. Cut Tafelspitz into thin slices, against the fibers.
8. To serve, place on a plate and pour with some soup. The Tafelspitz should always be covered with soup; otherwise, it will dry out. Garnish with chives and carrots.

WIENER SCHNITZEL
(viennese breaded pork cutlet)

Serves 4

SCHNITZEL

4	pork cutlets, pounded	¼	cup all-purpose flour
½	teaspoon salt	¼	teaspoon black pepper
2	large eggs	1	teaspoon whole grain mustard
½	cup breadcrumbs	½	cup oil
1	orange	2	tablespoon lingonberry
4	slices of fresh lemon		

HOW TO MAKE IT

1. To pound meat thinly, place the cutlet between sheets of plastic wrap for more comfortable washing up. Use a heavy, flat-surfaced pan to beat if you don't have a meat mallet. Pound the meat evenly to about a ¼ inch thickness.
2. Salt the meat on both sides with salt and pepper.
3. To bread the schnitzel, set up 3 shallow dishes: place the flour in one bowl, mix the egg with mustard and place it in the second dish, and the breadcrumbs in the third dish.
4. In a large skillet, heat at least 1/4-inch of oil to 350 F.
5. Working one at a time, dredge cutlets first in flour until the surface is completely dry; then dip in egg mixture to coat, allow the excess to drip off for a few seconds. Then roll quickly in the breadcrumbs until coated. Do not press the breadcrumbs into the meat. The crust should not adhere completely but form a loose shell around the schnitzel. Immediately place meat in the pan with the hot oil. Do not crowd the pan. Cook the schnitzel in batches, if necessary, for about 4-5 minutes. Turn to ensure both sides cook evenly.
6. Remove from pan, allow the oil to drain off, and serve with a slice of oranges topped with a ½ teaspoon of lingonberry; top with a lemon slice.

TRADITIONELLES RINDSGULASCH
(traditional hungarian beef gulash)

Serves 4

GULASCH

2	pound stew beef	2	large onions sliced
2	tablespoon oil	1	tablespoon Hungarian paprika hot
1	tablespoon Hungarian paprika sweet		
2	garlic cloves, minced	1	lemon, zested
1	teaspoon caraway seeds	2	tablespoon tomato paste
1	cup tomato sauce	2	cups beef stock
	Salt & pepper to taste		flour for thickening

HOW TO MAKE IT

1. In a large stockpot, heat oil on medium heat. Add sliced onion and sauté for about 10-12 minutes.
2. Add 2inch diced beef and roast for an additional 5 min. Add garlic and cook for 3 more minutes.
3. Add tomato paste and roast for about 3-5 minutes.
4. Add paprika, caraway seeds, and cook for an additional 3 minutes.
5. Deglaze with beef stock, bring to a boil.
6. Add tomato sauce and simmer for about 40 minutes or until meat is tender.
7. Remove all meat and with a small strainer sift the flour into the broth in small amounts while stirring until broth is thickened.
8. Place beef back into broth; add lemon zest and simmer for 10 minutes.
9. Season with salt and pepper to taste. Serve with buttered egg noodles.

 # JÄGER SCHNITZEL
(veal cutlet in a mushroom cream sauce)

Serves 4

SCHNITZEL

20	ounces veal cutlets	3	ounces olive oil
	flour for dredging	½	cup chopped onions
¼	cup chopped carrots	¼	cup chopped celery
2	cups red wine	1	cup veal or beef stock
1	tablespoon butter	2	ounces bacon diced
4	ounces pearl onions, boiled	2	cups wild mushrooms
2	tablespoon minced parsley		salt & pepper

HOW TO MAKE IT

1. Season the meat with salt and pepper, dip the pieces in the flour, and shake off excess.
2. In a medium sauté pan, heat 2 ounces of olive oil over high heat. Sear both sides of the meat until golden. Remove meat and set aside.
3. Add the onion, carrot, and celery. Sauté for 1 minute. Deglaze with wine and continue to cook until reduced by half. Add 3/4-cup of the stock and return meat to the pan, lower to a simmer, and cook until meat is tender.
4. Transfer meat to a plate and keep warm. Strain sauce. Reserve.
5. In another sauté pan, heat the remaining 1-ounce oil and butter. Sauté the bacon until golden. Add the pearl onions and mushrooms and continue to sauté until golden. Add to the sauce. Place the meat back into the sauce and simmer for 5 minutes
6. To serve, divide schnitzel into 4 portions on the center of heated plates. Pour the sauce with mushrooms and bacon on top. Sprinkle with minced parsley.
7. Serve with noodles.

 FORELLE AUF MÜLLERIN-ART
(fresh sautéed trout)

Serves 4

FORELLE

4	prepared whole trout	Salt, pepper to taste
¼	teaspoon lemon juice	flour for coating
6	ounce butter	Freshly chopped parsley or tarragon

HOW TO MAKE IT

1. Wash the fish in cold water and pat dry using kitchen paper. Season the stomach cavity with salt and pepper. Season the outside of the trout generously with salt and coat both sides in flour.
2. In a large pan, slowly melt half the butter (not allowing it to brown too much) and fry the trout on both sides, depending on their size, for a total of 12–18 minutes until crispy and golden brown (when turning the fish do not use sharp equipment, to prevent the skin from tearing).
3. Carefully lift the trout from the pan, arrange on pre-heated plates and keep warm by covering with foil (or by placing in a pre-heated oven on a low setting) discard any excess fat from the pan, add the rest of the butter and allow to bubble up before adding a generous squeeze of lemon juice. Add salt and allow to bubble up again. Drizzle over the trout on the plates and then sprinkle with the freshly chopped parsley.
4. Serve with potatoes coated with butter or parsley, accompanied by a seasonal salad. Instead of the whole fish, it is also possible to prepare fish fillets in this way.

SEMMELKNÖDEL
(salzburger bread dumplings)

Serves 6

SEMMELKNÖDEL

12	ounces of white old bread	1	cup milk hot
1	tablespoon butter	¾	cup diced onion white
4	each bacon strips, diced	2	each egg large
3	tablespoon minced parsley	1	teaspoon salt
¼	teaspoon pepper black ground	¼	teaspoon nutmeg ground
	breadcrumbs as needed		

HOW TO MAKE IT

1. Cut the crispy rolls/bread into small cubes; place into a medium bowl and pour hot milk over the bread; cover and set aside.
2. Cut bacon into small strips and sauté until crispy; set aside.
3. In a medium sauté pan, heat the butter and sauté the onions until translucent; add the sautéed onion to the bread mixture.
4. Add eggs, cooked bacon, parsley, salt, pepper, and nutmeg.
5. Knead the mixture together with your clean hands until all ingredients are thoroughly combined. When the mixture is to wet, add some breadcrumbs.
6. Wet your hands to prevent the dough from sticking and form Knödel about the size of a tennis ball (they will expand slightly when cooked). Press the Knödel between your palms to make sure they're nice and compact. Bring a large, wide pot of lightly salted water to a very light simmer - **not boiling** but just on the verge of boiling with tiny fizzy bubbles floating up. Carefully drop the Semmel Knödel in the water and let them "steep" 15-20 minutes. Do not let the water boil, or you risk your Knödel losing shape or falling apart. Carefully lift them out with a slotted spoon and serve hot!

WIENER GEFÜLLTE PAPRIKA
(stuffed bell peppers)

Serves 4

GEFÜLLTE PAPRIKA

4	red peppers	.5	pound potatoes
4	shallots, cleaned, chopped	.5	pound kielbasa sausage
4	tablespoon parmesan cheese	½	cup sour cream
2	eggs	1	teaspoon marjoram, finely chopped
2	tablespoon parsley, chopped	½	teaspoon soy sauce
1	tablespoon capers, chopped	6	ripe tomatoes
2	tablespoon sugar	2	fresh bay leaves
6	tablespoon oil for frying	3	tablespoon pork fat or olive oil
	salt, pepper, caraway seeds and ground nutmeg for taste		

HOW TO MAKE IT

1. Wash the peppers and cut off the caps. Remove the seeds and white flesh. Remove these from the caps of the peppers and cut a round lid.
2. Cut the potatoes in 4 mm cubes and sauté with shallots in the olive oil. Season with salt, pepper, caraway seeds, and nutmeg and add about 300 ml of water. Steam for about 10 minutes. When the water has evaporated, add the sausage.
3. Stir in the sour cream, marjoram, parsley, capers, egg and cheese, and season with pepper and salt. Fill the peppers with the mixture, push down well, and place the lids on top.
4. Brush the peppers with dripping or oil and place them on an ovenproof pan or dish. Mash together the tomatoes, sugar, bay leaves, salt, and a shot of Tabasco and add to the dish. Preheat the fan-forced oven at 365 °F and bake for 40-50 minutes. While the peppers are baking, stir the sauce repeatedly. When the peppers are tender, remove from the oven and place on a warmed plate. Purée the sauce and let simmer for a little longer if necessary. Pour over the stuffed peppers.

SCHWEINEMEDAILLIONS WITH CHAMPIGNONS
(pork medallions with mushroom sauce)

Serves 4-6

SCHWEINEMEDAILLIONS

2	pounds pork tenderloin	3	tablespoons olive oil
4	tablespoon butter	2	shallots, finely chopped
14	ounces mushrooms (cremini)	1	tablespoon all-purpose flour
½	cup red or dry masala wine	½	cup chicken stock
3	tablespoons heavy cream	¼	cup chopped parsley
	Salt and pepper for taste		

HOW TO MAKE IT

1. Trim the tenderloins of any excess fat. Cut the fillets into 2-inch-thick medallions. Flip each medallion onto a cut side and press down with the palm of your hand to flatten. Season the pork with salt and black pepper.
2. Heat the olive oil and 1 Tbs. of the butter in a large sauté pan over high heat. When the butter is melted and foaming, add half of the meat and sear until nicely browned, 2 to 3 min. Flip and cook the other side until the meat is well browned and slightly firm to the touch, about another 2 min. Transfer to a plate and repeat with the remaining pork.
3. Melt the remaining 3 Tbs. butter in the pan. Add the shallots and a pinch of salt and sauté for about 30 seconds, using a wooden spoon to scrape up any browned bits from the bottom of the pan. Add the mushrooms and sauté until the mushroom liquid has evaporated and the mushrooms are golden about 3 min. Season with 1/2 tsp. salt, sprinkle with the flour and add the Marsala.
4. When the Marsala has almost completely evaporated, add the chicken broth, and reduce by half, about 3 min. Stir in the cream and parsley, return the pork and any accumulated juices to the pan, and cook, flipping the pork once, until it's firm to the touch and still a little pink in the middle (cut into a piece to check), 2 to 4 min. Taste for salt and pepper and serve.

ZWIEBELKUCHEN
(onion and cheese quiche)

Serves 4

ZWIEBELKUCHEN

3	cups all-purpose flour	2.5	cups butter
3/8	cup cheese curd	3	egg yolks
1	pound onion chopped	.5	pound bacon finely cut
4	tablespoon scallions	½	cup leeks
8	tablespoon olive oil		salt and pepper to taste

FILLING

5	eggs	1	cup heavy cream
½	cup cheese (your choice)		salt, pepper and nutmeg for taste
	Butter for greasing the pan		

HOW TO MAKE IT

1. For the pastry, mix flour, butter, cottage cheese, egg yolks and a pinch of salt. Quickly knead until smooth. Wrap in plastic and refrigerate for 4 hours.
2. Halve the onions and slice. Heat the olive oil in a pan. Sauté the onions (without the spring onions), stirring them quickly until they are transparent. Remove from heat and allow to cool. Preheat the oven to 200 °C (400F). Grease the cake form with butter. On top of a floured surface, roll out the dough with a rolling pin about 4mm thick and place in the tray so that about 1 inch of it hangs over the edge.
3. Distribute the onions equally over the dough.
4. For the filling, whisk the eggs and the cream. Cut the leek and spring onions (only the white part) into rings and mix into the egg mixture with the bacon and cheese. Pour over the pastry.
5. To form a beautiful crust, use thumb and forefinger to shape the edge of the pastry around the edges of the tart form. Bake for about 40 minutes. Remove from the oven and leave to sit for about 10 minutes before cutting

KRAUTFLECKERL
(austrian pasta with caramelized cabbage)

Serves 4

KRAUTFLECKERL

1	white onion	1	head of white cabbage
2	ounces of sugar	1	teaspoon caraway seeds
2	ounces butter	1	pound pasta
6	ounces of bacon	2	tablespoon parsley chopped
1	glove of garlic chopped		salt and pepper to taste
1	tablespoon oil		

HOW TO MAKE IT

1. Slice bacon into small pieces.
2. In a medium sauté pan, heat the oil and crisp bacon. When crisp set aside.
3. Cut the cabbage (white, without a stalk) into squares, cut onion finely, and chop garlic.
4. Caramelize the sugar, and the caraway caramelize in a big pot. Now add the half of the butter, the onion, and the garlic, stir. Add the cabbage, salt, and stir.
5. Add the bacon and let it steam for about 30 minutes with a closed lid.
6. Fill a big stockpot with water and bring to a boil, add salt and cook the pasta until al dente.
7. Strain, rinse in cold water, and allow it to drain well. Chop parsley. Mix the pasta with the cabbage and stir. Add the rest of the butter and season with parsley and pepper. Serve while still warm.

KÄRNTNER GEBRATENER LACHS
(carinthian roasted salmon)

Serves 4

GEBRATENER LACHS

4	5 ounce pieces of fresh salmon	2	tablespoon olive oil
2	tablespoon chopped chives	1	tablespoon tarragon leaves
	Salt and pepper to taste	4	lemon wedges for service

HOW TO MAKE IT

1. Preheat oven to 425°F.
2. Rub salmon pieces all over with 1 teaspoon oil and season with salt and pepper.
3. Roast, skin side down, on a foil-lined baking sheet in the upper third of oven until fish is just cooked through, about 12-14 minutes.
4. Cut salmon in half crosswise, then lift flesh from skin with a metal spatula and transfer to a plate.
5. Discard skin, then drizzle salmon with oil and sprinkle with herbs and a lemon wedge.

TIROLER GEBRATENES HUHN
(tirlolian fried chicken)

Serves 4

GEBRATENES HUHN

1	pound chicken breast and thighs	1	cup of breadcrumbs
1	cup of flour	2	beaten eggs
1	teaspoon whole grain mustard		lemon juice
1	small rosemary spring		Oil for deep frying
2	ounce clarified butter	½	lemon, juices
	Salt and pepper to taste		lemon wedge for service

HOW TO MAKE IT

1. Cut the chicken into 2-inch pieces and season with salt and pepper.
2. Preheat a deep pot of oil or a deep fryer to 350 degrees F.
3. Bread the chicken pieces by first dredging in flour, then dipping in beaten eggs-mustard mixture, and lastly, rolling in breadcrumbs. Deep-fry in oil until done and golden in color. Drain off excess oil. Season with salt and squeeze fresh lemon juice.
4. In a small saucepan, heat the butter and rosemary just until warm. Allow to cool for a few minutes. Strain into a sauce bowl. Stir in lemon juice.
5. Skewer each piece in a rosemary sprig. Arrange in a serving platter, serve with Lemon Rosemary Butter Dipping Sauce, and garnish with lemon wedges.

 ESTERHAZY ROSTBRATEN
(vienna royal roast beef)

Serves 4

ROSTBRATEN

4	6 ounce beef tenderloins	2	each onion sliced in strips
1	medium carrot julienne	½	celery root cut julienne
1	small turnip, cut julienne	1	teaspoon capers
4	ounce bacon, cut into strips	4	tablespoon sour cream
1	tablespoon four for the sauce	1	tablespoon flour for coating
12	ounces beef stock		lemon zest
3	tablespoon butter		chopped parsley for garnish
	Salt and pepper to taste		

HOW TO MAKE IT

1. Cut the roast beef into inch-thick slices. If needed, truss each slice with butcher's twine to help them retain their shape during braising.
2. Season both sides of the beef generously with your salt and pepper. Next, dredge one side of your beef with flour.
3. In a medium sauté pan, heat your butter over high heat, then place your beef floured side down into the pan and sear for 2-3 minutes.
4. Flip your beef and sear that side for 2-3 minutes as well, then take out of the pan and set aside.
5. Add in your shallots and lightly brown them in the same pan for 2-3 minutes, adding some more butter as needed.
6. Deglaze the pan with your water or beef stock and reduce your stovetop heat to a simmer.
7. Place the slices of beef back into the pan, add just enough stock to cover the beef 2/3 to the top.
8. Cover your pan and braise the meat for about an hour or until tender.
9. Check periodically on the level of your braising liquid, adding more stock or water as needed.

CONTINUED

10. Heat a medium sauté pan over high heat and add your bacon, allowing it to render off some of its fat. As the fat renders, add in your chopped vegetables and sauté briefly for 3-4 minutes.
11. Add a dash of beef stock, then let the vegetable steam until 'al dente' for another 6-10 minutes.
12. In a medium bowl mix up a slurry of flour and sour cream (make sure your mixture is clump-free)
13. Once the beef has finished braising and is tender, take it out of the pan.
14. Using the same pan, the meat was cooked in, over low-medium heat, pour in the flour/sour cream mixture, stirring continuously for 1-2 minutes until it's thick and smooth.
15. Fold in your capers and lemon zest, then allow the sauce to reduce for another 3 minutes.
16. Next, put your Esterhazy Rostbraten back into the pan coating it evenly with the sauce.
17. When plating, arrange the beef slices on a plate and garnish with the sautéed root vegetables, some sauce, and fresh chopped parsley. Serve with pasta or fried potatoes and enjoy!

KÄRNTNER GEBRATENER LACHS

Christian J. Fischer

DESSERT

WIENER SACHERTORTE

APFELSTRUDEL

KAISERSCHMARRN

 WIENER SACHERTORTE
(viennese sacher torte)

Serves 4

SACHERTORTE

5	ounces salted butter	5	ounces dark chocolate
4	ounces powder sugar	6	large eggs
4	ounces all-purpose flour		apricot jam

ICING

6	ounces chocolate	4	ounces coconut shortening

HOW TO MAKE IT

1. Preheat the oven to 385°F.
2. Melt chocolate and butter in a double boiler over hot water (Bain Marie, "im Wasserbad"). If you do not have a double boiler, you can also use a standard pan filled with water and with a smaller pan in it.
3. Remove from heat and let the mass cool.
4. Add the powdered sugar and the egg yolks little by a little while carefully stirring. Beat the egg whites and add the white sugar. Mix into the batter and add the flour gradually while constantly stirring.
5. Pour batter into a greased springform pan. Bake at 350°F for 50 to 60 minutes.
6. Allow the cake to cool completely before removing from pan and before icing. Once cool, remove the cake from pan then slice horizontally. Insert a filling of pureed jam between the layers.
7. ICING: Melt chocolate and coconut shortening in a double boiler over hot water and cover the top and sides of the cake with the warm (not hot) icing.
8. Serve with fresh whipped cream.

 # FLÜSSIGER SCHOCOLADEKUCHEN
(lava cake)

Serves 4

SCHOCOLADEKUCHEN

4	ounces salted butter	6	ounces dark chocolate
3	egg yolks	2	large eggs
½	cup sugar	2	tablespoon all-purpose flour

HOW TO MAKE IT

1. Preheat the oven to 450°F.
2. Butter and lightly flour four 6-ounce ramekins. Tap out the excess flour. Set the ramekins on a baking sheet
3. In a double boiler, over simmering water, melt the butter with the chocolate. In a medium bowl, beat the eggs with the egg yolks, sugar and salt at high speed until thickened and pale.
4. Whisk the chocolate until smooth. Quickly fold it into the egg mixture along with the flour. Pour the batter into the prepared ramekins and bake for 12 minutes, or until the sides of the cakes are firm but the centers are soft. Let the cakes cool in the ramekins for 1-2 minute, then cover each with an inverted dessert plate. Carefully turn each one over, let stand for 10 seconds and then unmold. Serve immediately. You can serve it with ice cream or whipped cream and fresh berries.

 ÖSTERREICHISCHE APRIKOSEN KNÖDEL
(austrian apricot dumplings)

Serves 4

APRIKOSEN KNÖDEL

¼	cup cream cheese	1	large egg
4	tablespoon semolina flour	3	tablespoon breadcrumbs
1/3	cup all-purpose flour	2	tablespoon sugar
¼	teaspoon salt	8	small apricot
8	cubes of sugar	2	tablespoon salted butter
¾	cup breadcrumbs	1	tablespoon sugar
	Cinnamon to taste		powder sugar for dusting

HOW TO MAKE IT

1. To start, mix all dough ingredients with a fork until you get a nice smooth batter. It's slightly soft, but it will firm up when chilling in the fridge. Chill the mixture covered for at least half an hour. An hour or longer is even better since the dough is easier to work with when cold.
2. Wash apricots and pat them dry. It's easiest to pit them by inserting the back of a cooking spoon or spoon from one side (where the stem is) and pushing it out the other way.
3. Replace the apricot kernel with a sugar cube.
4. In a sauté pan, heat the butter. When melted, add the breadcrumbs, sugar, and a pinch of cinnamon if you like. Toast the breadcrumbs, often stirring, until golden. Don't forget about that residual heat, which can quickly burn your crumbs.
5. Take the dough out of the fridge and divide it into 8 portions on a well-floured surface.
6. Tightly wrap the dough around the apricot, sealing the edges and shaping it into a ball. If the side isn't sticking since you used too much flour, dip your finger in water and wet it to close the dough around the apricot.

CONTINUED

1. Ensure you don't trap any air inside, or the dumpling will not sink to the bottom of the pot as it is supposed to but will float from the beginning. (I always have a floater or two, no biggie, but it's better if they are sinking since the dough is cooked correctly, and the chance of bursting is lower.)
2. In a large pot, bring water to a boil. Cook the apricot dumplings for about 15 minutes in lightly simmering water (no rolling boil!) – they should float towards the end.
3. Remove the dumplings with a slotted spoon and transfer them to the pan with the breadcrumbs. Roll the dumplings in toasted breadcrumbs. Dust them with confectioners' sugar if you like.
4. Serve hot and Enjoy!

TIROLER BLAUBEERNOCKEN
(tyrolian blueberry dumpling)

Serves 4

BLAUBEERNOCKEN

14	ounces blueberry	4	ounces wheat flour
3	ounces milk	3	ounces sugar
2	tablespoon butter		pinch of salt
1	teaspoon powder sugar	2	ounces sour cream

HOW TO MAKE IT

1. Wash and pat dry the berries. Add a pinch of salt, some flour, and milk, combine carefully; try not to spoil the berries. Fold in flour and milk until the berries are stuck together. The consistency should be wet and soft (not runny). The less dough, the better. The berries will release their juices; you shouldn't drain them; they will substitute milk. That means, that we first add part of the flour and a pinch of salt. It's great if the berries are stuck without milk, if they aren't, add some milk.
2. In a medium sauté pan, melt enough butter to cover the bottom of the pan. When the butter starts foaming, drop dollops of dough into the pan.
   Sprinkle each dumpling with a fair amount of sugar (approx. 1/2-2/3 tsp per each). When we turn them over, the sugar and berry juices will caramelize together, which is the main secret of this dish!
3. Cook on one side. The berries will release juices making dumplings darker in color. Turn them over and sprinkle with sugar.
   At this stage the berries will release a lot of juices, the sugar will melt, and the dumplings will cook in berry caramel, sort of.
4. Dust with confectioner's sugar and top with sour cream to serve, or, for a more festive variation, top with sour cream or whipped cream, confectioner's sugar, and or vanilla.

 KÄRNTNER TOPFENSTRUDEL
(carinthian cream cheese strudel)

Serves 4

TOPFENSTRUDEL

1	sheet of puff pastry dough	3	tablespoon butter
3	tablespoon sugar	2	egg yolks
1 ¼	cup of curd or cream cheese	4	tablespoon sour cream
1	teaspoon lemon peel	2	egg whites
3	tablespoon raisins		flour for worktable
	Powder sugar for service		

HOW TO MAKE IT

1. Preheat the oven to 350F.
2. Beat the egg whites until very stiff in a medium chilled mixing bowl, set aside.
3. In another mixing bowl, mix butter until it's "fluffy" (it should be at room temperature, but not liquid)
4. Add sugar, cream cheese, sour cream, lemon peel, and raisins, add the beaten egg whites very carefully in the end.
5. On a table spread a little flour to roll out the puff pastry dough, about 3 millimeters.
6. Pour the filling on two-thirds of the strudel dough and fold in the edges. Very carefully roll the strudel.
7. Place the rolled strudel on a greased baking sheet.
8. In a small bowl, beat the egg yolks and brush the top of the strudel.
9. Bake in the oven for 45-60 minutes at 350F.
10. Sprinkle with powder sugar for service.

SPANISCHE WINDTORTE
(spanish meringue cake)

Serves 4

WINDTORTE

8	large egg whites	½	tablespoon cream of tartar
1	pound powder sugar	1	ounce lavender fondant
1	ounce purple fondant	1	ounce yellow fondant
4	large egg whites	2	cups powder sugar
2.5	cups heavy cream	½	cup strawberries, cleaned, sliced
10	ounce raspberries fresh	8	ounce pitted cherries

HOW TO MAKE IT

1. Line 3 large baking trays with baking parchment. Draw 2 x 20cm (8 in) circles on 2 of the trays and 1 x 20cm (8 in) circle on 1 of the trays. (You should end up with 5 x 20cm (8 in) circles). Preheat the oven to 250F.
2. For the meringue shell, tip the egg whites and cream of tartar into a large spotlessly clean bowl and whisk with an electric mixer on high speed until the whites form stiff peaks. Add the caster sugar, a tablespoon at a time, whisking continuously to make a thick, glossy meringue.
3. Spoon two-thirds of the meringue into a piping bag fitted with a 1.5cm (⅝ in) plain nozzle. Pipe a thick ring inside one of the circles on the baking tray and continue spiraling until the entire circle is filled. Repeat with a second circle. These create the base and the top of the meringue cake.
4. Repeat the process with the 3 remaining circles, except don't fill in the circles, so that you have three hoops of meringue - these create the sides of the meringue shell. Bake for 45 minutes. Remove from the oven and leave to cool.
5. Meanwhile, make the fondant violets. For each fondant violet, roll 2 little pieces of dusky lavender fondant and 3 small pieces of deep purple lavender into small balls (about the size of an orange pip). Dust 2 pieces of greaseproof paper with icing sugar and place the balls of fondant between the sheets of greaseproof and flatten each ball out with your fingers, to a thin circle, approximately 1cm (½ in) in diameter - these form the petals.

CONTINUED

Greaseproof and flatten each ball out with your fingers, to a thin circle, approximately 1cm (½ in) in diameter - these form the petals. Roll a tiny piece of yellow fondant into 3 tiny balls to form the stamens.

6. Using a small paintbrush and a tiny amount of water, stick the petals and stamens together to form a violet, with the 2 dusky lavender petals at the top, 2 dark purple petals below them and the remaining dark purple petal on the bottom, in the middle. Press the yellow stamens into the center. Repeat to make 13 violets. Leave to dry on greaseproof paper for at least 1 hour.
7. When the meringues are dry, gently slide 1 of the cooked, filled meringues onto a 30cm (12 in) heatproof (to 248F) serving plate. Spoon the remaining meringue into the piping bag and pipe 8 blobs of meringue, evenly spaced around the edge of the circle. Place 1 of the meringue hoops on top and press down very gently to stick the hoop to the base.
8. Repeat the process with the remaining 2 hoops of meringue. Roughly pipe the remaining one-third of meringue around the sides to disguise the hoops. Using a spatula smooth out the meringue so that the sides are smooth and straight and look like a cake. Bake for 45 minutes. Remove from the oven and leave to cool.
9. For the Swiss meringue decoration, set a large mixing bowl over a pan of gently simmering water. Tip the egg whites and sugar into the bowl and whisk until the sugar is dissolved and the meringue reaches 158F on a sugar thermometer.
10. Remove from the heat and continue whisking until cool and stiff. Spoon the meringue into a piping bag fitted with a large star nozzle. Pipe a pretty border around the base, the middle, and the top edge of the meringue shell. Pipe a border around the outside edge and the center of the filled meringue circle that will become the lid. Bake for 30 minutes. Remove from oven and leave to cool.
11. For the filling, whip the cream and icing sugar together in a bowl until soft peaks form when the whisk is removed from the bowl. Whisk in the orange blossom water and gently fold in the strawberries and raspberries. Spoon into the cooled meringue cake shell. Top with the meringue lid.
12. To decorate, use tiny blobs of meringue to stick 6 violets around the middle-piped border on the sides of the cake, 6 violets around the top of the cake, and 1 violet in the center of the top of the cake. Serve immediately.

WACHAUER MARILLENKNÖDEL
(apricot dumplings)

Serves 4

MARILLENKNÖDEL

12	ounces quark	8	ounces all-purpose flour
2	ounces butter	1	packet vanilla sugar
1	fresh egg	10	small fresh apricots
10	sugar cubes	4	ounces breadcrumbs
4	ounces butter	½	teaspoon cinnamon
2	tablespoon powder sugar		pinch of salt

HOW TO MAKE IT

1. Cream the softened butter with vanilla sugar and a pinch of salt. Add the egg, quark, and flour and knead into a pliable dough. Shape into a ball, wrap in film and leave to rest in a cool place for 30 minutes.
2. Wash the apricots, remove the stones and place a sugar cube instead. On a floured working surface, shape your dough into a roll 2 inch thick. Slice the roll into approximately ten equally sized slices, then take each slice and gently flatten it between your hands.
3. Place an apricot into the dough and seal it by pressing the dough all around the apricot. To get the dumpling perfectly round and well-sealed, roll the dumpling between your hands as if you're trying to form a ball. Prepared dumplings place on a floured surface.
4. Fill a large saucepan with slightly salted water and bring to the boil. Lower the heat, transfer the dumplings to water, and leave them to simmer slowly for 10-13 minutes. Stir the dumplings to prevent them from sticking together.
5. To make the garnish, fry breadcrumbs in butter until golden yellow, flavor them with cinnamon, add sugar at the end.
6. When cooked, carefully remove the dumplings from water and roll them in the prepared garnish. For serving, arrange on plates and dust with powder sugar.

ÖSTERREICHISCHER APFELSTRUDEL
(austrian apple strudel)

Serves 6-8

APFELSTRUDEL

1	sheet frozen puff pastry, thawed	1	teaspoon ground cinnamon
2	large fuji or gala apples, sliced thin	1	lemon, juiced
½	cup raisins	½	cup sugar
2	tablespoon butter	½	teaspoon vanilla
1	small egg		flour for worktable
	powder sugar for service	1	spring of fresh mint for service

HOW TO MAKE IT

1. Position an oven rack in the center of the oven and preheat to 375F.
2. In a medium bowl, toss the sliced apples with the lemon juice, cinnamon and vanilla until the apples are thoroughly coated. Add the raisins, ½ cup sugar, and the 2 tablespoons cold cubed butter and toss well. Set aside.
3. Lightly dust the counter or work surface with flour. Lay the puff pastry on top and dust the rolling pin with additional flour. Gently roll the puff pastry to 1/4-inch thickness.
4. Spread the apple and raisin mixture over the bottom half of the puff pastry square leaving about 1-inch of space along the side edges. Fold the top half of the puff pastry over and pinch to seal the edges together.
5. In a small bowl, beat the egg, brush the entire strudel evenly with the beaten egg. With a fork, diagonally puncture the strudel to let steam escape when baking.
6. Place the strudel on a parchment-lined baking sheet and bake for 40 minutes, rotating halfway through cooking, until the pastry is puffed and golden brown
7. Serve with fresh mint, powder sugar.

HELLE LINZER PLÄTZCHEN
(linzer cookie)

Serves 12

LINZER PLÄTZCHEN

4	ounces butter, room temperature	¾	cup confectioners' sugar
¼	teaspoon almond extract	1	cup all-purpose flour
1	large egg	½	cup raspberry or red currant jam
	Confections sugar for dusting		

HOW TO MAKE IT

1. In a medium bowl, cream 4 ounces room-temperature butter with 3/4 cup of confectioners' sugar and 1/4 teaspoon of almond extract. Add the egg.
2. Stir 1 cup of all-purpose flour into the creamed ingredients and knead just until mixture forms a ball.
3. Wrap the dough in plastic and refrigerate for 30 minutes.
4. Heat oven to 350 F. Line a cookie sheet with parchment paper.
5. Dust work surface with confectioners' sugar and roll out cookie dough to about 1/8-inch thick. Using a Linzer cookie cutter, cut an even number of bottoms (without the cutout) and an even number of tops (with a hole in the middle). Transfer with a spatula to the prepared cookie sheet.
6. Bake for 10 to 12 minutes. Remove from the oven. Let cool on cookie pans for a few minutes. Then remove to wire racks to cool completely
7. Sift confectioners' sugar over the cooled cookie tops (the ones with a hole) and set aside. Spread the bottom half of the cooled cookies with 1 teaspoon jam of choice. Immediately place a dusted cookie top on the jam-coated bottom cookie and press lightly to adhere.

ERDBEER SCHOKOLADENKUCHEN
(strawberry chocolate cake)

Serves 4

ERDBEER SCHOCOLADEKUCHEN

2 ½	cup white sugar	2	cup all-purpose flour
1	cup unsweetened cocoa	3	eggs
1 ½	teaspoons baking powder	1	teaspoon salt
1 ½	teaspoons baking soda	1	cup milk
½	cup vegetable oil	1	teaspoons vanilla extract
1	teaspoon almond extract	1	cup boiling water
1	cup strawberry jam		

FROSTING

2	cups heavy cream	2	tablespoon sugar
2	pounds fresh strawberries		

HOW TO MAKE IT

1. Preheat the oven to 350°F. Grease and flour two 9-inch round baking pans.
2. In the mixing bowl, stir together sugar, flour, cocoa, baking powder, baking soda and salt in large bowl. Add eggs, milk, oil, almond and vanilla; beat on medium speed for 2 minutes. Stir in boiling water (batter will be runny). Pour batter into prepared pans.
3. Bake 30 to 35 minutes or until wooden pick inserted in center comes out clean. Cool 10 minutes; remove from pans to wire racks. Cool completely
4. While the cake is cooling, make the frosting. In the bowl of a mixer, beat the heavy cream and sugar on medium speed until fluffy; do not overwhip.
5. To assemble the cake, cut the cake into three rings, place one cake on a cake stand. Spread first the jam, then the frosting over the bottom layer of the cake. Next, slice 1 cup of strawberries lengthwise and place them on top of the frosting. Carefully place the second cake on top of the strawberries and gently press down to help set the cake. Repeat for the third layer. Spread the final frosting over top of the cake and cover with the remaining strawberries. Serve immediately.

ÖSTERREICHISCHE PFIRSICHPLÄTZCHEN
(austrian peach cookie)

Serves 4

PFIRSCHPLÄTZCHEN

1	cup white sugar	¾	cup vegetable oil
½	cup milk	2	eggs
¾	teaspoon baking powder	¾	teaspoon vanilla extract
3 ½	cups all-purpose flour	1	cup apricot or peach preserve
½	cup almonds	3	ounce cream cheese
2	tablespoon tea powder	2 ½	tablespoon brandy
¾	teaspoon ground cinnamon	¼	cup red decorating sugar
½	cup orange decorating sugar	2	cups baking crumbs

HOW TO MAKE IT

1. Preheat the oven to 325°F.
2. Combine sugar, oil, milk, eggs, baking powder, and vanilla in a large bowl. Blend in enough flour to form a soft dough.
3. Roll into golf ball size balls. Place an on ungreased cookie sheet.
4. Bake for 15-20 minutes. Cookies will be pale. Remove to a rack to cool.
5. Hollow out cookie center. Reserve crumbs. Combine 2 cups crumbs, preserves, almonds, cream cheese, instant tea powder, brandy and cinnamon. Mix to blend.
6. Fill cookies with crumb mixture. Press 2 cookies together to form one peach.
7. Brush lightly with brandy or water and dip one spot in the red sugar for blush and the roll entire cookie in orange sugar. Top with an icing leaf or purchase the plastic peach leaves and impress your family and friends.

ÖSTERREICHISCHE SCHOKOLADENBÄLLCHEN
(austrian chocolate balls)

Serves 40

SCHOKOLADENBÄLLCHEN

2	ounces unsweetened chocolate	½	cup butter
1	cup white sugar	2	eggs
½	teaspoon almond extract	1 ½	cups all-purpose flour
½	cup chopped walnut or cashews	1	ounce unsweetened chocolate
½	teaspoon vanilla	1	tablespoon butter
1	cup confectioners' sugar	3	tablespoon milk

HOW TO MAKE IT

1. Preheat the oven to 350°F.
2. In a small saucepan over low heat, melt 2 ounces of chocolate with ½ cup of butter. Stir frequently until melted; remove from heat and set aside to cool.
3. In a medium bowl, mix sugar, egg, egg yolk, and almond extract until light and fluffy. Stir in the melted chocolate. Combine flour and walnuts and stir into the batter until just combined. Shape dough into 1 inch balls and place them 1 inch apart on ungreased cookie sheets. If the dough is too sticky, refrigerate for 30 minutes before forming balls.
4. Bake in the preheated oven for 10 to 12 minutes, or until firm to the touch. Transfer to wire racks immediately and set aside to cool.
5. In a small saucepan over low heat, melt 1 ounce of chocolate and 1 tablespoon butter together, stirring frequently until smooth. Remove from heat and stir in vanilla and confectioners' sugar until well blended. Beat in the milk one tablespoon at a time until the glaze is of the desired consistency. Dip the tops of the cookies into the glaze and allow to dry completely before storing in an airtight container.

KAISERSCHMARRN
(the king's pancake)

Serves 4

KAISERSCHMARRN

4	large eggs, divided	3	tablespoon butter, melted
1	teaspoon vanilla extract	2	tablespoon sugar
1	pinch of salt	1	cup of all-purpose flour
1	cup milk		

FOR THE SOAKED RAISINS
1/3	cup raisins	3	tablespoon rum

TO CARAMALIZE
2	tablespoon sugar	2	tablespoon butter
2	tablespoon confectioners' sugar to serve		

HOW TO MAKE IT

1. In a small bowl, combine raisins and rum.
2. Separate the eggs and set the egg yolks aside.
3. In the bowl of a stand mixer fitted with the whisk attachment, add the four egg whites and beat at high speed about 2.5 minutes until stiff peaks form. Transfer to a bowl and set aside.
4. Add the four egg yolks, melted butter, vanilla extract, sugar, and a pinch of salt to the (now empty) bowl of your stand mixer, still fitted with the whisk attachment. Combine at medium speed about 2-3 minutes.
5. On low speed, alternately add flour and milk, a tablespoon of each at a time, until you used up the milk and the flour. Don't overmix. Scrape down the sides and up the bottom of the bowl as needed.
6. Using a metal spoon or rubber spatula, fold in the stiff egg whites until combined, and no big egg white lumps remain. You need to be very gentle and light-handed. Don't over mix.
7. Heat 1 tbsp butter in a 12-inch skillet over medium heat. Pour the batter into the skillet and cook for about 6-7 minutes.

CONTINUED

8. After 3 minutes, sprinkle the drained raisins over the batter. Use a spoon to peak under the pancake to see if it's golden brown underneath.
9. When the pancake is golden brown underneath, sprinkle the top with a little bit of sugar. Using a spatula, divide the pancake into quarters and turn the pieces. Add a little bit of butter to the pan while turning the pancake.
10. Cook for 3-4 minutes until the quarters are golden brown underneath.
11. Using two spatulas, tear the pancake into bite-sized pieces.
12. Add 2 tbsp butter and sprinkle 2 tbsp sugar over the pancake pieces. Turn up the heat to medium-high and gently toss the pieces with a spatula for about 3-4 minutes, until the sugar has caramelized.
13. Sprinkle with confectioners' sugar and serve in the pan with applesauce on the side.

WACHAUER MARILLENKNÖDEL

FLÜSSIGER CHOCOLATEKUCHEN

ERDBEER SCHOCOLADEKUCHEN

HELLE LINZER PLÄTZCHEN

ABOUT THE AUTHOR

Christian J. Fischer began his love affair with Austrian food growing up in his family's businesses and when he became a chef/baker/butcher apprentice in Bad Gleichenberg at the age of thirteen. His trips to the markets of Austria sparked a lifelong obsession with authentic local meats, spices, great desserts and all kinds of local fruits and vegetables. In 1988, when he became the Chef of his first restaurant, he was one of the first to combine the flavors of traditional Austria with French technique. The restaurant was a sensation, immediately earning four stars, and launching his career which led him to work all over the world, own his own restaurants and cook for presidents and royalty.

Now, Christian J. Fischer has brought together the best of his Austrian recipes in one exciting cookbook. The recipes reflect Christian's extraordinary talent for creating intensely flavorful dishes inspired by his diverse cultural experience and simple home cooking. He loves cooking for, entertaining and sharing his culinary knowledge with his family and friends and now is excited to share his passion with the world. He lives in Connecticut with his loving wife in their antique home built in 1775. He has 4 beautiful children, 3 whom were adopted from China, which has furthered his diverse culinary flair as he brings together all their heritage flavors of northern and southern China, New England and all with an Austrian Twist.

From taste-tempting appetizers, soups, and salads, to irresistible fish, meat, poultry, and vegetable dishes, to unique sauces and one-of-a-kind sweets, the recipes in *"For The Love Of Austria"* promise to make dining at home as exciting as an evening out at any of the historic towns of Austria or Christian Fischer's own dining room table.

REFERENCES

(Austria.org, n.d.)
(History of Austria, n.d.)
(Austrian Salt World, n.d.)
(Taste of Austria, n.d.)
(Wikipedia Austria, n.d.)

INDEX

SOUPS
    FRITATTENSUPPE — Pg. 25
    LEBERKNODELSUPPE — Pg. 26
    GULASCHSUPPE — Pg. 27
    WIENER KARTOFFELSUPPE — Pg. 28
    BLUMENKOHLSUPPE — Pg. 29
    APFEL – SELLERIESUPPE — Pg. 30
    CHAMPIGNONCRÈME SUPPE — Pg. 31
    KÜRBISCREMESUPPE — Pg. 32
    GRIESSNOCKERLSUPPE — Pg. 33
    WIENER ZWIEBELSUPPE — Pg. 34
    KNOBLAUCHCRÈMESUPPE — Pg. 35
    RINDSSUPPE — Pg. 36

SALADS
    WARMER ERDÄPFELSALAT — Pg. 43
    GURKENSALAT — Pg. 44
    TOMATENSALAT — Pg. 45
    WARMER KRAUTSALAT — Pg. 46
    GRÜNER BOHNENSALAT — Pg. 47
    SPARGELSALAT MIT WACHTELEIER — Pg. 48
    GRÜNER SALAT MIT FRESCHEN BIRNEN — Pg. 49
    EVDIVIESALAT MIT APFEL — Pg. 50
    TOMATENSALAT MIT AVOCADO — Pg. 51
    MELONENSALAT MIT PROSCIUTTO — Pg. 52
    RÜBENSALAT MIT APFEL — Pg. 53
    RETTICHSALAT MIT KÜRBISKERNEN UND KÜRBISÖL — Pg. 54
    ROTKOHLSALAT MIT APFEL UND WALNÜSSEN — Pg. 55
    FRISCHER GEMÜSESALAT — Pg. 56

SIDE DISHES
    AUSTRIAN SPÄTZLE MIT KÄSE UND ZWIEBELN — Pg. 63
    TIRLOER GRÖSTL — Pg. 65
    HABSBURGER SCHWAMMERLGULASCH — Pg. 66

WIENER GEDÜNSTESTER ROTKOHL	Pg. 67
KRAUTSTRUDEL	Pg. 68
EIERNUDELN MIT GERÖSTETEN SCHWAMMERLN	Pg. 69
ÖSTERREICHISCHER WEISSER SPARGEL	Pg. 70
STEIRISCHE SPÄTZLE	Pg. 71
CHAMPIGNON UND PILZ RISOTTO	Pg. 72

ENTRÉES

ÖSTERREICHISCHER TAFELSPITZ	Pg. 70
WIENER SCHNOTZEL	Pg. 80
TRADITIONELLES RINDSGULASCH	Pg. 81
JÄGER SCHNITZEL	Pg. 82
FORELLE AUF MÜLLERIN-ART	Pg. 83
SEMMELKNÖDEL	Pg. 84
WIENER GEFÜLLTE PAPRIKA	Pg. 85
SCHWEINEMEDAILLIONS WITH CHAMPIGNONS	Pg. 86
ZWIEBELKUCHEN	Pg. 87
KRAUTFLECKER	Pg. 88
KÄRNTNER GEBRATENER LACHS	Pg. 89
TIROLER GEBRATENES HUHN	Pg. 90
ESTERHAZY ROSTBRATEN	Pg. 91

DESSERTS

WIENER SACHERTORTE	Pg. 99
FLÜSSIGER SCHOCOLADEKUCHEN	Pg. 100
ÖSTERREICHISCHE APRIKOSEN KNÖDEL	Pg. 101
TIROLER BLAUBEERNOCKEN	Pg. 103
KÄRNTNER TOPFENSTRUDEL	Pg. 104
SPANISCHE WINDTORTE	Pg. 105
WACHAUER MARILLENKNÖDEL	Pg. 107
ÖSTERREICHISCHER APFELSTRUDEL	Pg. 108
HELLE LINZER PLÄTZCHEN	Pg. 109
ERDBEER SCHOKOLADENKUCHEN	Pg. 110
ÖSTERREICHISCHE PFIRSICHPLÄTZCHEN	Pg. 111
ÖSTERREICHISCHE SCHOKOLADENBÄLLCHEN	Pg. 112
KAISERSCHMARRN	Pg. 113

Made in the USA
Middletown, DE
20 September 2020